WRITE FOR MONEY AND POWER

THE ANTI-STARVING ARTIST'S GUIDE TO BECOMING A SEVEN-FIGURE WRITER

AMY SUTO

For the writers who want it all

CONTENTS

INTRODUCTION: A MANIFESTO FOR WRITERS WHO WANT MONEY AND POWER

If you picked up this book, chances are you already love writing.

You write because it rewired your brain, helped you survive a breakup or a dead-end job, or because stories have always whispered louder than reality. You write because you *have* to. That's great, and the baseline for what it takes to succeed as a writer. However, what you're about to read isn't about writing for love. That's a given, and not something I can teach you.

No, this book is about how to write for *money and power*.

Because the problem with most writers isn't talent. It's scale. You've got the skill. What you need now are the mindset and models that reinforce your belief that, yes, you can build a seven-figure writing career—and no, you don't need gatekeepers to do so.

Why This Isn't Another Freelancing Guide

Write for Money and Power was never meant to be a sequel. When I sat down to expand on the ideas behind my previous book *Six-Figure Freelance Writer*, I thought I was writing an extra chapter or two. I was planning to pen a continuation of tactics for people who wanted to earn more from their writing, and to summarize the lessons that took my writing career from six figures to seven. But as the pages filled, it became clear I wasn't writing a handbook. I was tearing out the blueprints.

What you're holding now is something entirely different. Instead of a guidebook for freelancers, this is a full operating system upgrade. Not just for how you write, but for how you think about writing as a vehicle for wealth, autonomy, and power.

Most writing advice assumes your goal is publication. This book? Well, I'm going to assume your goal is liberation. *Freedom.*

Because what good is another productivity tip or pitch template if the entire mental model you're operating from was designed to keep you broke? What good is knowing how to "build a brand" if you still believe you must starve for your art?

This isn't "freelance writing for dummies." It isn't "monetize your creativity in three easy steps." This book is a *reckoning*.

Yes, we'll talk about business models—how to structure your ghostwriting rates, paid newsletter ecosystems, and self-publishing strategies. But the real transformation begins long before the tactics. It begins in the rewiring of belief systems that told you writing and money should never share a sentence. That told you power belonged to someone else. That said you had to suffer for your art to earn legitimacy.

I wrote *Write for Money and Power* to blow the ceiling off your creative limits. It's built to spark the kind of perspective shift that can realign your entire writing career, just like certain books on business, psychology, and craft once did for me. (You'll also find some of my book recommendations listed in the back, in case you're ready to keep the momentum going once you finish reading.)

My goal is to stretch the limits of what you think is possible, especially if those limits were handed to you by outdated systems or self-serving members of the old guard who never wanted you to have leverage in the first place.

The Writers This Book Is For

This book is for both fresh-faced beginners and grizzled experts. Because in my experience? Beginners and experts often wrestle the exact same demons.

The names change: imposter syndrome, burnout, panic, or the worry that "what if this all disappears tomorrow?" Underneath it all, the fear is the same: *I'm not ready. I'm not enough. I can't charge that. I'll never get hired again.*

That script is the problem. And I'm here to rewrite it.

Even if you have a perfect website, a snappy bio, or a buzzing client funnel, none of that matters if you can't confidently get on a call and pitch your rate. You won't go anywhere meaningful if you're scared to put your name on a book, or hit publish, or ask to be paid what you're worth.

So we're starting where success actually begins. Because when your mind is in the right place, action becomes inevitable. The next steps appear. The right clients show up. Your pricing finally starts to match your potential.

And if you do want the more tactical, step-by-step how-to guide, that's what *Six-Figure Freelance Writer* was built for. You can grab the e-book for 99 cents from your retailer of choice and keep it as your tactical toolkit. Think of that book as the field manual, while this book is the command center.

The Method to the Madness

Write for Money and Power will show you the exact methods that built my career. Will following them guarantee you seven figures? No. Because there are no guarantees in life. Just death, taxes, and your laptop crashing right before a big deadline.

What I can tell you is this: in my ten years as a freelance writer, these are the truths I wish had been obvious. Instead, I had to dig them up through trial, error, and a generous helping of late-night existential dread.

I'm writing this for you, yes. But I'm also writing it as a service to the younger version of myself. The writer who didn't know what she didn't know. The one who kept refreshing her inbox, hoping the right opportunity would magically appear. This is what I wish someone had handed me ten years ago. Five years ago. Even just a year ago.

To get here, I've made every expensive mistake in the book. I've undercharged, overdelivered, burned out, and walked straight into traps I now see coming a mile away. I've spent tens of thousands of dollars in missed opportunities, poor decisions, and painful lessons. I'm writing this to help you avoid the potholes and literal cliffs I had to tumble down in order to learn what I know now.

The framework I share in these chapters is built on three income pillars that work together to support your creative freedom: paid newsletters, self-published books, and freelance writing. On their own, each of these can be powerful. But when you align them, they become a system that builds both income and independence. Most writers treat these areas like separate silos. In reality, they're deeply interconnected. And when you learn to build them in sync, each one helps accelerate the others.

A paid newsletter (often hosted on platforms like Substack or Beehiiv) gives you steady income and a direct relationship with your readers. It's a space to test ideas, share your voice, and start charging for your in-progress thinking. It can also become a testing ground for a future book.

A self-published book gives you something to sell. It's your intellectual property. It earns while you sleep. It helps your newsletter audience go deeper and gives you the chance to build long-term assets instead of waiting on publishers or agents.

Freelance writing, especially at the luxury level, gives you high-ticket income that funds everything else. It pays the bills while you build your audience. It also becomes easier to book clients when you can point to a published book or a thriving newsletter as part of your portfolio.

This system is what helped me grow my writing business. And now it's here to support yours.

As you move through this book and explore how to bring these three pillars into your world, remember that this system is adaptable. I'll be sharing what worked for me, but you might be working toward something different. For example, I built my writing business to prioritize two things: taking care of my health and having the freedom to travel. I've written from rooftop apartments in Barcelona, cabins in Nashville, and too many cafes in Seoul to count. That was the life I wanted. But your ideal day might look nothing like mine. Maybe you want to write quietly from your home office, with a dog at your feet and no airport security in sight. Maybe you're raising young kids or caring for aging parents or balancing a full-time job while slowly building your writing business on the side. All of that is valid.

The goal isn't to chase someone else's version of success. It's to build a writing business that funds the life of your dreams. So if I'm talking about flying to Kyoto for a writing sabbatical, and you're thinking about saving for your kid's college fund or building enough margin to take weekends off, just swap my dream for yours. The structure still holds. Power doesn't necessarily equal passport stamps. Money doesn't mean luxury. It means *choices*. And if this system gives you more space for the people and things you care about, then it's already working.

After you've finished reading, I can't promise you fame, fortune, or inboxes full of dream clients. But I can promise that everything of value I've learned, built, tested, and refined over the last decade is in these pages because I believe in paying it forward. And these words are me sending that goodwill your way.

How I Got Here

I didn't start writing with power in mind. I started with panic.

Fresh out of USC film school, I landed the dream first rung on the ladder: a Hollywood assistant gig working under big names. I fetched green juices, tracked red carpet RSVPs, and took script notes from people who hadn't read the scripts. I told myself I was lucky. That this was the price of entry.

When I finally clawed my way into a TV writing room, I had a writing credit and a seat at the table and was still dipping into savings to pay rent even as I had an episode of TV with my name on it.

Everyone around me said the same thing: "Be patient. Pay your dues. Wait your turn."

Except I'd done everything "right" and I was still broke, still burned out, still begging the same gatekeepers who handed out scraps with a smile.

Then came the real turning point: I was diagnosed with an autoimmune disease.

It happened shortly after I went all-in on freelancing. I had walked away from Hollywood, from the career path I was "supposed" to want, and instead of crawling back to the assistant ladder, I was choosing myself. But then my fingers started swelling. Typing became painful. The very thing I'd staked my livelihood and identity on— writing—was now the thing making me cry at my keyboard.

And then came the moment that changed everything.

It was 2021, in the thick of COVID. I was sitting in the waiting room of my first rheumatologist's office, waiting for answers. A woman walked in, visibly in agony. Her joints were so stiff she couldn't even hold the pen to sign her name on the check-in form. I watched her try, my heart hurting for her. I watched her choke back tears as she begged the front desk to be seen early, that her rheumatoid arthritis flares were worse than ever. And I remember thinking: *Is this my future?*

I was diagnosed with rheumatoid arthritis that day. And I knew in my bones, and in the joints that were already betraying me, that I couldn't wait on an industry to save me. I couldn't gamble my health on "maybe someday" or "pay your dues" or "when you're lucky enough to get staffed again." I needed to write in a way that paid my medical bills now. I needed to rewrite my business model in a way that didn't break my body.

So I stopped doing what I'd always done: overextending, overdelivering, overcommitting. I got ruthless. Fewer clients. Higher rates. Clearer boundaries. Systems that served my health, not the hustle.

It wasn't easy. Rheumatoid arthritis is one of the most expensive autoimmune diseases to treat. I spent tens of thousands of dollars out-of-pocket. I fainted after that first blood draw, lying woozy on the exam table, overwhelmed by the magnitude of what I was facing, not just physically, but financially. And in the beginning of my journey, I had doctors who weren't committed to helping me before I found the ones who could. One doctor even refused to run the iron panel I asked for, until I fought back. When the results came in, the deficiency was severe. I had to learn how to advocate for my health while also learning how to advocate for my writing.

But I'll go ahead and skip to the good part: I got better.

I found functional medicine practitioners who listened. I overhauled my routines. I scaled back my hours while scaling up my income. I prioritized healing, and in the process, I rebuilt a writing career that didn't depend on traditional institutions or 12-hour days.

And now? As of writing this, I'm in full remission. Off medication. Stronger than I've ever been. I've hiked the 26-mile Inca Trail to Machu Picchu. I take boxing classes for fun. I climb stairs for pleasure when just a few years ago, I could barely walk without wincing.

Write for Money and Power isn't just a guide to making money as a writer. It's about finding your personal power and wielding writing as the tool that helps you take it back.

Now, I live in my dream home in San Francisco, surrounded by forests and sunlight. I ghostwrite memoirs for founders and other inspiring individuals across different continents. My paid newsletters clear six figures a year. My self-published books (like the one you're reading now!) fund both passion projects and plane tickets. I've watched the sun rise over Cappadocia, taken month-long writing sabbaticals in Florence, and booked flights to China simply because it sounded fun.

These pages are here to tell you that it's okay to want more. Because more is possible. Not in some vague "follow your dreams" poster way, but in the form of actual business models, pricing frameworks, sales scripts, and systems.

We'll get there by reprogramming every outdated script in your head that says money is selling out and power is for someone else.

And let's be clear: I'm not talking about fake power. Not a title. Not a meager book deal that undervalues your talent. Not a screenwriting job where someone else owns your best ideas.

I'm talking about power in the form of *true freedom.*

The ability to write what you want, when you want. To never set an alarm clock unless it's for an international flight. To bankroll your life, your travel, your boldest ideas. *That* kind of power is real. And it's learnable, even if you're a complete beginner.

If you've ever felt the pang of wanting more—money, impact, freedom—welcome. Let's turn that fire into strategy.

Chapter One starts with the lie that keeps most writers broke.

And then we burn it down.

PART I

YOUR MINDSET
MAKEOVER

1

THE LIE THAT KEEPS
WRITERS BROKE

Picture this: Rome, 1508. The Sistine Chapel is a dusty construction zone. Fresco pigment thickens the air. Scaffolds groan. And Michelangelo, paint-streaked, exhausted, allegedly cranky as hell, isn't there working because of divine inspiration. He's there because the Pope backed up a (proverbial) Brinks truck.

He didn't work for "exposure." He wasn't "grateful just to be chosen." The Vatican paid him 3,000 ducats, the modern equivalent of hundreds of thousands of dollars, and he negotiated every damn detail.[1] Payment schedules. Assistants. Materials. Timeline. The man even submitted line-item receipts.

Now stop and let that sink in: the artist we've been told was perpetually starving was operating as a contractor, not a beggar.

By the time he died, Michelangelo had accumulated a fortune that, by some conservative reconstructions, would be worth more than £30 million (over $35 million USD) in today's money.[2] That

---

1. Gerry Martinez, "Did Michelangelo Get Paid to Paint the Sistine Chapel?" *Gerry-Martinez.com*, accessed September 30, 2025, https://www.gerrymartinez.com/did-michelangelo-get-paid-to-paint-the-sistine-chapel/
2. John Hooper, "Michelangelo's Sistine Chapel Paintings Were Work of Suffering

number doesn't square with the image you've been sold of the tortured genius eating stale bread in a rundown candlelit room. Instead of being a beggar, Michelangelo was stacking gold like a Medici side hustle, using his image to his advantage.

The starving artist narrative didn't start in the Bohemian cafés of Paris. It was PR, and you were never the customer. You've always been the product.

How I Got Suckered Into the Lie

I was twenty-two, underpaid, triple-shot latte in hand, working phones at a rising literary agency in Hollywood—headset on, heart cracked open with ambition. This was supposed to be the first rung of the ladder on the way to my dream. I had done everything right: graduated from USC's screenwriting program, landed an assistant job inside the system, and spent my days juggling call sheets and lunch orders for the power players who made the dreams happen.

From the outside, I looked "in." From the inside, I saw the rot. Even as I moved on from that job and got deeper into the industry, I saw established writers unable to pay their credit cards. Some lost their homes in the turmoil of industry politics and show cancellations, even if they had storied credits and had contributed to fancy shows that raked in money for the executives running the show.

The strategy was simple: keep writers dazzled by proximity to power. Give them a backlot badge, a fancy title, a tiny windowless office with a named parking spot as a consolation prize. Dangle the illusion of prestige just long enough to keep them broke, grateful, and obedient.

It worked, and now the income of writers in Hollywood is crumbling with the outdated system. According to the Writers Guild of America, screenwriter earnings and employment declined by 6%

Genius," *The Guardian*, accessed 2025, https://www.theguardian.com/world/2002/nov/30/artsandhumanities.arts

during the first three quarters of 2024, and the number of working screenwriters decreased by 15%, compared to 2022.[3]

I had a front-row seat to the collapse long before the trades caught up. One of the most surreal moments came while I was working on a glossy, high-profile series. Our writers' room was in a mansion in the Hollywood Hills with marble countertops, panoramic views of Los Angeles, and catered lunches on the patio. It felt like we'd all made it.

And then the show got canceled.

Just like that, the illusion cracked. The contracts ended. The emails stopped. And every writer in that room—people with real credits, real talent, years in the game—began scrambling to figure out how they were going to make rent, pay for health insurance, keep their kids in daycare. The despair hit fast and quiet. We threw some big parties on our way out of that mansion, but I saw the fear underneath the champagne toasts.

Because when you don't control distribution, you don't control your livelihood. That wasn't a bug in the system. That was the system working exactly as designed.

You can have the Hollywood Hills zip code, the buzzy show, the glittering IMDb page—and still lose everything overnight. The dream isn't real if you can't own it. And what most writers think is power is just rented status. Real power is building something that doesn't disappear when the mansion empties out.

I met the writers I thought I wanted to become. Quietly, behind closed doors, they told me what it actually cost. The medical debt. The NDAs. The creative compromises. The ten years it took to get one pilot made, and then how the network buried it.

Meanwhile, your team all takes a cut of your earnings, even if you get a job yourself. Studios and publishers are constantly looking to trim budgets, and writers are the easiest line item to squeeze because

---

3. Writers Guild of America West, *Writer Employment Snapshot*, accessed 2025, https://www.wga.org/uploadedfiles/the-guild/reports/WGA_Writer_Employment_Snapshot.pdf

of the damaging starving artist lie you've accepted. They'll steer you toward the project with the widest audience appeal, not the one that actually lights you up. Because their incentives aren't yours.

Some of the highest-paid creatives in Hollywood can't get their own projects made. Francis Ford Coppola reportedly had to borrow over $100 million against his own wine business to fund his movie *Megalopolis*.[4] If he has to mortgage his wine empire to chase autonomy, what does that say about the rest of us?

Meanwhile, the studios run Hollywood accounting so a blockbuster that grosses hundreds of millions can legally post a loss, stiffing the creatives on net-profit bonuses.[5]

No More Waiting

You're told to wait patiently for a book deal, a staff job, a producer who finally "gets it." And in that waiting room, your audience is slipping through your fingers. Your best work collects dust in a sad file on your computer while you hope someone on a studio lot returns your email.

I've been inside the machine you think you want to be part of. And I'm telling you: it's not built for you. It's not here to serve you. The people within it might be kind, even brilliant—but the system itself is not designed to make you rich, powerful, or free. It's meant to benefit the people at the top.

It's designed to keep you grateful. It's designed to keep you waiting.

And if you think it'll all be worth it once your show gets made or your book hits shelves, remember that traditional publishing often takes two to three years to launch a manuscript. Screenwriting time-

4. Stephen Galloway, "Francis Ford Coppola Funded His $120 Million Film 'Megalopolis' with His Wine Business," *Business Insider*, accessed 2025, https://www.businessinsider.com/francis-ford-coppola-funded-megalopolis-100-million-wine-business-2024-9

5. Wikipedia contributors, "Hollywood Accounting," *Wikipedia*, accessed 2025, https://en.wikipedia.org/wiki/Hollywood_accounting

lines are worse. You could sell a pilot tomorrow and wait five years for it to air, if it ever does. 99.9% of purchased scripts are killed before they reach a film set. Sometimes your story might even be taken away from you and given to another creator to make instead.

If you want money and power, you cannot afford to give your voice, your future, and your platform to people who see you as a line on a spreadsheet.

And if you're still not convinced, that's okay. You may need to walk the road and see for yourself if it's worth it. Who knows? Maybe the slot machine will turn in your favor. Maybe you'll get the big deal, the dream job, the *New Yorker* review (which, by the way, you can still get if you self-publish your book). But even if you win, you still don't own your audience.

And when the machine gets tired of you, or the project tanks, or your name gets overwritten, what's left? You've bought lottery tickets with your precious time and energy, and if the odds aren't in your favor you have nothing to show for it.

No email list. No reader connection. No platform you control.

I've seen it happen. I've lived it up close. And I'm here writing this because I don't want that fate for you. You don't need to beg the machine to feed you anymore.

You can build something of your own. You can own both your words *and* the revenue, reach, and resonance they create.

You just have to stop seeking approval from gatekeepers and start building.

The Middleman Math

Let's talk about the math they hope you never run. Because once you do, the whole house of cards starts to wobble.

Middlemen aren't just gatekeepers. They're margin-thieves dressed like opportunity. And they count on your creative dream blurring your financial vision.

Time to fix that.

TV Staffing: The Mirage of Momentum

Staff writer on a hit show? Sounds glamorous. And for a few months, it might be.

Minimum pay on a WGA contract (as of 2025) starts around $5,069 a week. Not bad, until you realize:

- You're only paid during the room's duration (maybe 10 weeks, but the actual length of a writers' room has shrunk in recent years due to cost-cutting measures at studios).
- You'll owe 10% to your agent, 5% to your lawyer, and maybe another 10-15% to your manager, which comes off your gross earnings (aka: your pre-tax cash).
- Your checks can be delayed months while your agency assistant fires off endless "just checking on status" emails to business affairs.
- Your intellectual property, otherwise known as IP? Gone. You don't own what you write, the network does.
- Oh, and that deal you signed? It likely includes exclusivity or a first-position clause, meaning if another show wants to hire you, you can't say yes unless the scheduling aligns perfectly—or unless the original show releases you, which they often won't.

So yes, $50,000 for 10 weeks might hit your account. And then? You could go 12, 18, even 24 months (or longer!) without another staff job. You still don't own your rights, your audience, or control over your destiny.

That's not a business model. That's a very fancy cage. Power lies with the person who holds the keys to your dream, and if you don't take them back, you'll be begging for every step in your writing career journey.

Book Deals? More Like Book Debt

[OBJ]Meanwhile, the publisher owns your copyright and decides whether your book gets a paperback, an audiobook, or a pulse. (Spoiler alert: just because your book is being published with a big imprint does not mean you'll ever see it in hardcover!)

I know what you're thinking: book deals are heralded as the goal of many writers. A six-figure advance feels like champagne money. Pop the cork, right? Slow down: that check isn't a paycheck. It's a liability stamped "recoupable," which is industry speak for debt. Until your royalty statements claw back every dollar, you're working off the balance like a junior associate pulling all-nighters for the partners upstairs. Not to mention that a big book deal trumpeted as seven figures can dribble out in five installments over four years while 15% flies to the agent before your taxes hit.[6] [7]

Even with a $50,000 advance, which sounds great on paper, you might end up with less than $30,000 after your agent and taxes. Then subtract your launch budget, because you'll be footing the bill for personal publicity and extra book marketing unless you're a marquee name.

And if that book doesn't "earn out"? Good luck getting a bigger advance next time.

Think of the book deal contract as a bank note with your talent as collateral. The publisher takes a mortgage out on your future pages. In return, you get a lump sum now, but they now own the house. Miss a deadline or ask for a structural rewrite and they can hold the next payment hostage. They can even call in the loan by demanding repayment if you walk away. That's not freedom. That's indenture wrapped in a congratulatory email.

The recoupment math rarely lands in the author's favor. Most

---

6. Mary Adkins, "How Much Do Authors Make?" *Mary Adkins Blog*, accessed 2025, https://maryadkinswriter.com/blog/how-much-do-authors-make
7. PublishDrive, "What Are Book Advances? How Book Advances and Royalties Work," *PublishDrive Blog*, accessed 2025, https://publishdrive.com/what-are-book-advances-how-book-advances-and-royalties-work.html

books never "earn out." Returns, discounts, and confusing royalty math drain your momentum before the book even breaks even. If the book falls short, you may keep the advance, but good luck negotiating a higher one next time. Your sales track record is tattooed on your ISBN for every editor to see.

Meanwhile, you've traded your autonomy for the privilege of being someone else's employee. Cover design you hate? Tough. Marketing plan that consists of a single post from the publishing house account? Smile and reshare. Launch date shoved a year and a half out because a celebrity memoir cut the line? Send another grateful email and shuffle your PR roadmap.

Contrast that with self-publishing. Upfront costs are yours, but so are the royalties, the rights, and the timeline. You decide whether to price your book at $4.99 or $24.99. You choose the audiobook narrator. You pivot on a Tuesday because the market shifts. No overpaid executive can kick your work into oblivion.

Understand that a book deal is book *debt*, just an unsecured loan with creative strings and a velvet-lined cage. If you're chasing wealth and freedom, independent publishing (otherwise known as self-publishing) is the way to go, but we'll cover how to approach publishing like a creative entrepreneur later in this book. This is the path where *you*—not an overworked publishing exec in Midtown decrying the downfall of the martini lunch—hold the deed to your writing life.

The Indie Path: Where the Math Actually Works

Let's look at the flipside: the ownership path. This is a trio of creative, profitable business models that let you take full control. Self-publishing. Paid newsletters. Freelancing. Each one gives you leverage, speed, and ownership in a way traditional systems simply don't. We'll go deeper into all three later in this book—but for now, here's a quick overview of how they work and why they're worth building your creative business around.

. . .

Self-Published Book

You keep the copyright. You decide the timeline, price point, cover, and content.

Print-on-demand platforms like Amazon KDP or IngramSpark take approximately 30% and in exchange, they:

- Print and ship your book.
- Handle returns.
- Deliver global distribution on major book buying platforms.
- Offer distribution to libraries, bookstores, and universities.
- Allow you to see your sales in real-time.

They don't own your work. They don't touch your ownership. And if you want to scale up later and print in bulk with your own fulfillment setup? You can, and you'll reduce your per-unit costs, write those expenses off, and keep even more margin. Yes, they take somewhere around 30% depending on your setup with them. But they do the heavy lifting, and they don't sit on your rights. In this case, you're outsourcing logistics without sacrificing ownership.

Paid Newsletter

- You own your audience and your email list is yours forever.
- You control cadence, topic, offer, and pricing.
- Fees range from 2.9% to approximately 10% depending on the hosting and payment platform, and you get paid fast. Sometimes on the same day.

No agent. No exec. No delay. Just value, offered directly, and money in your account before the espresso finishes dripping.

. . .

Freelance Writing

Unlike Hollywood or trad-pub contracts, you write the terms.

- Want 80% upfront? Ask for it.
- Want a kill fee and two-round revision limit? Add it.
- Want to work async from a yacht off the coast of Croatia? Cool—it's your contract.

Freelancing lets you:

- Set your own rates.
- Choose your clients.
- Scale based on your bandwidth, not a studio's budget.
- Cancel or renegotiate terms on your schedule.

When you understand the value you bring, you can build a career around non-refundable deposits and flexible deliverables—not begging a studio for the rest of your check 18 months after you turned in a script they never shot.

Why the Lie Persists

The starving artist myth survives because it benefits the middlemen. Here's how:

- **Scarcity Economics.** If writers believe income is about "luck," they undercharge on principle. They work for "exposure." They treat pay as a bonus, not a baseline.
- **Romance of Suffering.** Starvation is rebranded as purity. Poverty becomes a badge of honor. As if your rent is supposed to be paid in vibes. Why do you think Hollywood and the publishing industry portray so many writers as broke and starving in a way that paints the suffering as romantic?

- **Institutional Bloat.** Layers of agents, assistants, retreats, and catered lunches have to get paid. Guess who absorbs the cost of your agent's $100 lunch with one of a hundred network execs they might meet with that year? Or a quarterly retreat for the office? (Spoiler: it's you.)

Michelangelo laughs from his marble tub.

Your Wake-Up Call

It took me years to realize that words are leverage. Writing is capital. Your stories are real business assets. And when you treat your career like you're the CEO of your destiny, the whole damn game flips.

- You can self-publish your next book and grow a reader base so loyal they sell it for you, one ecstatic review and social post at a time.
- You can start a paid newsletter about the topics you never shut up about and turn it into a six-figure subscription business just by being yourself.
- You can ghostwrite a memoir for a high-profile founder and earn more from one book than most authors see in a decade, allowing you to fund your freedom and creative projects.

But only if you let go of the discount-dance mentality.

You are not a typist. You are not a starving poet waiting for a call from an agent who stopped reading slush piles a decade ago.

You're a strategist. A tastemaker. A founder of a one-person writing empire if you choose to be. More on this in *Chapter Eight: "Becoming a Creator CEO."*

What Comes Next

In the chapters ahead, we're going to torch every leftover scarcity script they slipped into your head and replace it with systems, strategies, and numbers that build real wealth.

We'll build a money engine that pays your rent, your private chef, and your month in Tuscany. I'll teach you how to build writing-based revenue engines that let you eat croissants in Paris at noon on a Tuesday without scrounging for time off.

We'll define what power means—not in fake titles, but in time freedom. Creative power. The ability to live, work, and thrive on your own terms.

Because the scandal isn't that writers want money and power.

The scandal is how long we've been told that we don't deserve them.

Power Move: Your Myth Detox Starts Now

Right now, write down the biggest number you've ever allowed yourself to imagine earning in a year from your writing.

Got it?

Now triple it.

That tight feeling in your chest? That's the myth leaving your body.

The rest of this book is about how to make that number feel like a warm-up.

Let's begin.

Amy's Field Notes: A Few Words from My Brownstone Era

In November of 2024, I spent most of the month in New York City living in a brownstone in Chelsea, right across the street from Brooklyn Bagel, which is home of (and this is not up for debate) the best bagel I've ever had in my life.

Each morning, I'd walk down my tree-lined street, order an everything bagel with egg, pepper jack cheese, and maybe avocado if I was feeling like it, then loop over to Starbucks for a hot chocolate. Then I'd return to the brownstone, sunlight pouring through the windows, vines curling up the brick, and I'd write.

That's where most of my romantasy novel *The Ash Trials* came to life. It was a dream stretch of time—the kind of writing season I used to think only existed for people with book deals and calendar invites from Important People. But here I was, in a city that built its legacy on literary gatekeeping, writing on my own terms. No greenlight from anyone but myself. No advance check tied up in a contract. Just me, my words, and the revenue stream I'd built around them.

So when I got invited to a Substack party on the Upper East Side —one of those invite-only salons for "bestselling" writers on the platform with 100+ paid subscribers—I said yes. I showed up to a wood-paneled, old-money kind of venue with *New Yorker* profiles hanging on the walls and waiters with silver platters boasting tiny hors d'oeuvres. But what struck me wasn't the setting. It was the *energy.*

Everyone in that room had figured out how to make writing their job. No one was waiting for a greenlight. These were writers with 100 or even 10,000 paid subscribers. These writers were making tens of thousands, even millions of dollars, because readers wanted to hear what they had to say—and were paying for the privilege.

There were no gatekeepers in that room. No one was simply handed their readership. Everyone there had *built* something. The gripes still existed, but under the jokes and the champagne flutes and the exchange of subplots and strategy was something far more powerful: personal power. These were self-made systems, self-decided paths. Everyone in that room had built their own version of literary success. For some, that was on top of past success, but there were many self-anointed writers in that room.

I left the event a little overstimulated, but buzzing with ideas. I hopped in a car and watched the Manhattan skyline pass by as I took stock of the writers I had engaged with that night. And I thought: *This is it. This is the future.*

Writers used to need publishers, producers, and institutions to validate them. Now we just need a laptop and the guts to hit "publish."

That's what this book is about. Not chasing crumbling institutions, but becoming undeniable without them.

You'll read about how to attract your true fans. How to own your platform. How to step into a new mode of power. One bagel sandwich, one subscriber, one chapter at a time.

2

WELCOME TO THE CREATOR ECONOMY: YOUR PERMISSION SLIP TO WANT MONEY AND POWER

W hen Mark Duplass stepped onstage to deliver the keynote at SXSW in 2015, he didn't waste time on small talk.

"The cavalry isn't coming," he told a room packed with aspiring filmmakers and industry insiders.

He wasn't being dramatic. He was naming a collective delusion—one that creative people across industries still cling to. The idea that if you just keep making good work, eventually someone in power will notice. That at some point in your career, you'll be discovered, rescued. That some industry veteran will appear with a golden ticket and say, *We've been waiting for you.*

That's the cavalry. And Duplass, a filmmaker, writer, actor, and indie trailblazer best known for co-founding Duplass Brothers Productions and steering the mumblecore revolution with *The Puffy Chair, Baghead, Cyrus, Jeff, Who Lives at Home*, and *The Do-Deca-Pentathlon*, was there to break the news: they're not coming.

He wasn't speaking from theory. This was a filmmaker who had built his career the old-school indie way: a $1,000 feature made with friends, followed by years of bootstrapped storytelling that turned into a string of cult-hit films. And yet, even with momentum, even with fans, even with traction—he kept waiting for the cavalry.

Duplass went on, "Your agent's going to call you and say, 'I know the first time I called you, I said the cavalry was coming, I was wrong. The second time I said the cavalry was coming, and I was wrong. But this time? The cavalry is fucking beating down your door.'"

But when they do come—*if* they come—they don't always bring what you need. And they rarely understand what you're trying to build. Duplass continued, saying there would be a good chance that "...you don't wanna make a movie with the cavalry because they don't make the kind of movies you like, and they're gonna try and tell you exactly how to make the movie."

This is the part no one warns you about. You spend years fighting for access to traditional systems, and by the time you get it, you may not want it. You may realize that the strings attached are too tight, the compromises too great, the version of success they're offering isn't actually yours.

Duplass had reached that point. He was tired. Tired of generating everything himself. Tired of hoping someone else would take the reins. And yet, standing there on that SXSW stage, he made peace with the truth:

"Who gives a fuck about the cavalry? Because now *you* are the cavalry."

This is the shift. The moment when a creator stops waiting and starts owning. He wrapped up his talk with this line: "If you can accept that the cavalry won't come and just make yourself into the cavalry, it has your best chance of maintaining success [...] and more importantly it gives you a chance to be happy."

His real message was about finding success on your terms, and creating your own source of happiness as the ultimate power move.

Duplass said all this in 2015, before the Creator Economy exploded. Before a writer could build a six- or seven-figure business from a newsletter. Before social media alone could crown authors into bestsellers. Before fan-funded novels, self-produced films, and creator-owned content became the smart bet instead of the fallback plan.

He figured it out ahead of schedule. And now, you don't need a $1,000 indie film to test the model. You just need Wi-Fi and a plan.

So if you're still waiting to be chosen, this is your invite to join the Creator Economy.

After all, you're not waiting for the cavalry anymore.

The Duplass Doctrine in Practice

Mark Duplass didn't wait for Warner Brothers to bless his script. He shot his film *The Puffy Chair* for $1,000 with borrowed gear, cut it on a laptop, and leveraged the buzz into a streaming deal that bought him the freedom ten studio general meetings could not. The cavalry wasn't coming, so he found freedom for himself and started marching other filmmakers through the gate he'd kicked open.

You may not own a RED camera or have a brother who directs, but you do own distribution channels unimaginable to creatives of the past.

The Creator Economy Is the New Land of Milk and Honey

One of the biggest entertainment moguls on the planet isn't a studio head or a billionaire's son. He's a guy from North Carolina who made YouTube videos out of his bedroom. MrBeast's billion-dollar empire started with a camera, an algorithm, and a relentless obsession with understanding attention. Now he's got a snack line, an Amazon deal, and a global fanbase who shows up the second he hits "upload."

That's not a fluke. That's the future.

The Creator Economy is projected to surpass $480 billion by 2027.[1] The platforms elites scoff at today will determine the new elites

---

1. Goldman Sachs, "The Creator Economy Could Approach Half a Trillion Dollars by 2027," *Goldman Sachs*, accessed 2025, https://www.goldmansachs.com/insights/articles/the-creator-economy-could-approach-half-a-trillion-dollars-by-2027

of tomorrow.

And writers? You've got the skills that power it—storytelling, clarity, emotional resonance—but many of you are still stuck pitching executives who ghost you instead of publishing directly to readers who pay you.

This chapter is here to embolden you to stop waiting and start building.

Naval Was Right: If You Secretly Despise Wealth, It Will Elude You

Writers are taught to love craft and loathe cash.

To feel like wanting "more than enough" is greedy. To believe that true art springs from pain—not from a fair exchange with readers willing to pay for our work.

Bullshit.

As investor and philosopher Naval Ravikant put it: "If you secretly despise wealth, it will elude you."[2]

If you treat money like the enemy, it'll believe you. If you believe writing for an audience is "selling out," your bank account will gather dust. Money is not evil. Money is *fuel*. And in the Creator Economy, fuel gets turned into freedom—faster than ever.

Reprogramming begins when you identify the voice in your head that says *more than minimum is greedy*. That voice is rarely yours. It is a parental caution, a professor's warning, an industry elder waving a mug emblazoned with the words PAY YOUR DUES. It is the anxious mutter of institutions terrified you might notice how little of the pie you are actually eating.

Replace it with a new baseline: money is fuel. Power is freedom. Fuel takes you off the hamster wheel of invoice-to-invoice survival. Power lets you decide whether to write at dawn in a Barcelona café, or whether you decide to take the day off to pick up your kid early

---

2. Naval Ravikant, "Play long-term games with long-term people," *X (formerly Twitter)*, accessed 2025, https://x.com/naval/status/1002103559276478464

from school and spend the day at Disneyland. Neither outcome requires a Lamborghini or a mansion in the Hills—unless that lights you up. The point of amassing money and power is *choice*.

Maybe you're still clinging to the myth that real artists suffer for their art, and poverty is part of that suffering. I used to believe it, too. I thought pain (in all of its forms) made my writing more raw. That chaos somehow sharpened the edge of my voice. But here's what actually happened: my work got sharper the moment I stopped suffering. When I got healthier, my sentences did too.

Don't take it from me, though: notorious filmmaker David Lynch who was known for his highly creative experimental films like *Eraserhead* and the paradigm-shifting show *Twin Peaks*, was against the "suffering for art" mentality. In his book *Catching the Big Fish: Meditation, Consciousness, and Creativity*, he states that "The more the artist is suffering, the less creative he is going to be." He goes on to say that "Anger and depression and sorrow are beautiful things in a story, but they are like a poison to the artist. You must have clarity to create."

I could fill an entire book with all the ways in which the suffering writer has been deified in society, but instead let's talk about how you can walk away from that myth and serve your creativity and your bank account at the same time.

The Shift: From Employee to Creator

I took a class at USC called *Writing to Be Read*. It was the first time anyone told me that writing wasn't just about personal catharsis, it was about connection. That class flipped a switch. I stopped writing for the mirror and started writing for the reader.

And let me be clear: writing for your audience doesn't mean betraying your voice and "selling out" for some machine. It means fine-tuning your impact. To do this, you'll need to find the overlap between what lights you up and what your audience is hungry for, and build from there.

MrBeast succeeded because he reverse-engineered human attention. He tests thumbnails. He optimizes every beat of his videos.

Writers can do the same with every paragraph, every page, every email subject line.

What keeps people reading? What earns their loyalty? What turns one click into a true fan?

That's the creator's mindset. And it's the key to your freedom.

You Only Need 10,000 True Fans

Back in 2008, Kevin Kelly published his now-famous essay: "1,000 True Fans." The premise is simple, and he writes that "To be a successful creator you don't need millions... you need only thousands of true fans." If 1,000 people buy everything you make (your books, your classes, your merch, a subscription to your paid newsletter) you don't need millions of followers. You need depth, not breadth, especially in the internet age.

Updated versions of this model show that with 10,000 buyers per year with $10 of profit per person means that you're making $100,000 annually. Raise the price, increase the value, deepen the connection, and suddenly you're on a seven-figure trajectory.

And before you say "but 10,000 people is a lot," let me ask you this: Can you find 10,000 English-speaking humans on the planet who like the same weird, wonderful things you do? Who would love the stories only you can tell?

Of course you can. And if you can't, you either have a distribution problem, or a product-market-fit problem.

Product-Market Fit for Writers (Sounds Technical, But Will Change Your Life)

In the startup world, "product-market fit" is when a good product meets a hungry market and everything clicks. For writers, your "product" is your book, your newsletter, or anything else you create. Your "market" is your audience.

Product-market fit happens when the thing you love creating also delivers something your audience desperately wants.

If you write poetry about robot bees that no one buys, you have two options:

1. Change how you market it. Maybe there's a sci-fi horror community that would eat it up.
2. Find the adjacent genre that you also enjoy writing and that readers are already spending money on.

The nice thing about living in the digital age (aside from never having to fax anything) is that we get real data about how our work is landing. Paid newsletters show open rates, click-throughs, and how many people are sticking around to actually pay you. Self-publishing? You've got dashboards with real-time sales and preorder numbers—no begging your publisher for a PDF from three months ago like it's a sacred scroll.

While you can't just tell stories based on data and trends, it does give you information about what's trending with the audiences you're reaching. This can help you get a clearer path for the next thing you publish.

This isn't about selling out. It's about showing up where your voice resonates most deeply.

Action Over Approval

You are one post away from a different life.

One scrappy essay. One self-published book. One short film uploaded in the dead of night. We are living in an era where a single creative act can rip through the algorithm and rewrite your future, yet most writers are still waiting for someone else to give them the go-ahead. Why? Because they've been trained to believe action is dangerous.

What if it's not good enough? What if it ruins your brand? What if only three people buy it and one of them leaves a review that says "mid"?

Here's what's actually dangerous: doing nothing.

While you debate your tagline, someone else is building a six-figure audience from their free fan fiction. While you second-guess your pricing, someone else is uploading their novel and waking up to a thousand preorders. While you're trying to appease a fake committee in your head, your real future fans are starving for what you haven't published yet.

You're not going to dilute your brand by showing up. You are going to starve it if no one sees your work.

The Creator Economy doesn't reward polish. It rewards participation. You've got to get in the game to play the game. There's no fancy velvet rope. The only cost of entry is the courage to hit "publish" and the willingness to keep improving in public.

Sometimes the post you barely edited becomes the one that changes everything. Sometimes the book you were least precious about becomes someone's favorite thing they've ever read. You can't predict what's going to resonate. You can only give it a chance to exist.

And yeah, someone might hate it. Might leave a snarky comment. Might roll their eyes in your group chat. But someone else is going to underline your sentences and whisper "finally."

This is the trade. The risk. The reward.

You can be the writer who keeps rewriting Chapter One. Or the writer who builds a business, a body of work, a reader base and an extraordinary creative life: one post at a time.

Your audience can't find you if you never show up.

So show up. After all, *you* are the cavalry.

Power Move: Study the Success Stories

Before you build your own story empire, go excavate the master plans from writers who already have.

For this Power Move, find three creators in the wild who are making serious money from their words without gatekeepers.

Head to a paid newsletter platform. Who's dominating the leaderboard? Who's charging $10/month to serialize fantasy novels or teach storytelling systems and has thousands of paying subscribers?

Pop open your favorite online bookstore. Look up bestselling self-published books in your favorite genre. Find the ones who aren't backed by a Big Five publisher but are pulling in thousands of glowing reviews.

Dig into social media. Not for vanity metrics, but for signs of a real ecosystem. Which writers are earning enough from serialized stories to quit their jobs, fund sabbaticals, or buy a beach house in Mexico?

Take notes. Screenshot anything that sparks something in you—a pricing model, a reader testimonial, a clever packaging strategy. This is your creator-competitor landscape, your evidence file.

And if you don't find anyone doing what you want to do? Even better. It means there is a sea of opportunities waiting for you.

Just be wary of creators or coaches trying to sell you shortcuts, because there's no "easy" way to do any of this. The path of least resistance is simply flowing in your authentic self and carving your own path, but you can take pointers from the world to see what resonates most with you.

You get to be the one who charts that map. The one who goes from zero to one. The one who others will be asking how you did it.

The Creator Economy rewards pioneers—especially the ones brave enough to stop lurking and start posting.

So study the greats. Then start your own empire and find your unique voice.

Amy's Field Notes: Royalties, Reader Emails, and Real Impact

I still remember the first time royalty money from a book I wrote just... landed in my bank account.

No invoice. No agent splitting the check. No studio middleman slicing off a cut. Just a deposit with my name on it because someone, somewhere in the world, decided that my words were worth paying for.

Back when I was in Hollywood, I wrote scripts that died on hard drives. Detailed characters, carefully plotted arcs, punchy dialogue—

all of it invisible, save the work I did for other people's shows. But my own scripts and original ideas? No one read them. No one wrote to me about them. They just evaporated into the ether of optioned-but-unmade content.

Now? I get emails from readers who found my romantasy book *The Ash Trials* at 10 p.m. on a Tuesday, devoured it by morning, and want to know when the next one is coming. From readers who used my book *Six-Figure Freelance Writer* as a launchpad to raise their rates and land their first $10,000 project, or who tripled their hourly rate and wrote to say thank you.

That's not a flex. That's the ripple effect.

I'm writing to you from a foggy San Francisco, working on this book as I still get royalties from the books I finished last year. Or the year before. My past writing funds my future life.

When I talk about money and power, this is what I mean. The ability to change your life (and someone else's!) with a book. To watch doors swing open not because you waited, but because you shipped.

This ripple effect is real. It's how strangers become superfans. How a page you wrote in solitude becomes a bridge to someone else's transformation. How you earn the fuel to fund your next big experiment.

I want you to feel that. Not once. Not by accident. But on purpose, again and again.

You don't need to be the next Hemingway. You need to be the first *you*—loud, unfiltered, and unafraid to let your work live in the world.

That's the power move—and your new mission.

3

DAILY RITUALS FOR
REWIRING REALITY

The last time I made a vision board that came true, I was standing barefoot in a sun-drenched hotel room in Madeira, Portugal. My partner Kyle and I had just thrown open the windows. Palm trees swayed in the salty wind, and the Atlantic shimmered like scattered coins. Every morning, sunlight poured in. Every night, we fell asleep to the soft hush of the ocean.

It felt like a portal. So we did what you do in sacred places: we made a plan.

Together, we created a vision board for our next chapter. We were thinking about moving to San Francisco as our last official stop on our digital nomad journey, but instead of just making a pro/con list or scrolling real estate sites, we also picked images. The kind of gym we wanted to belong to. The shape of our future office. The warm wood floors, the light fixtures, the couch. A life that felt both grounded and expansive.

Six months later, that entire vision board was our reality.

Same luxury gym right around the corner. Same kind of home we'd pasted into our future. I had even bought the same brand of standing desk as I had added in my vision board—and didn't even realize it until we had assembled it in my office!

At one point after making the vision board, I had considered that maybe Kyle and I would be happier living in New York, instead. But the vision board was too strong. The blueprint had already been built in my brain, and now we've built a lovely life here in San Francisco that feeds my soul on a deeper level than I thought possible. Every time I walk through the breathtaking tree-lined streets and quaint Victorian architecture that surrounds up my home, I know I made the right choice. But it wasn't just a choice: it was a bit of magic, too.

When I make vision boards now, I don't shrug them off as woo-woo nonsense. I treat them like future plans.

Because our reality builds what the mind rehearses.

Vision Boards: Training Wheels for Time Travel

Vision boards work because the brain is a magician that obeys rehearsal.

A 2025 study on "Digital Vision Boards in Goal-Setting and Reflection" found that students who reviewed their boards weekly hit significantly more milestones than the control group. Imagery doesn't just inspire you, it sharpens focus and boosts follow-through.[1]

Your brain doesn't know the difference between memory and imagination. When you feed it imagery of the life you want, again and again, your cortex stops labeling it fantasy and starts treating it like a template.

I made my vision board using a simple online graphic design tool (there are plenty you can choose from!) and set my vision board as my laptop wallpaper and as my phone's home screen.

Remember: repetition turns dreams into default settings.

---

1.   Emilia Santos, "Utilizing Digital Vision Boards in Goal-Setting and Reflection," *ResearchGate*, accessed 2025, https://www.researchgate.net/publication/391037151_Utiliz ing_Digital_Vision_Boards_in_Goal-Setting_and_Reflection

Journaling: The Mind's Maintenance Log

James Pennebaker's research shows that 20 minutes of expressive journaling for just four consecutive days can lower blood pressure, boost immune markers, and reduce doctor visits.[2] But beyond the health data, there's power in clarity.

Journaling helps me find business breakthroughs and is the "garbage collector" who takes out the trash of my mind. It helps me when I feel overwhelmed or unsure, which was quite often when I was reforming my beliefs around what it means to be a professional writer.

During a critical phase of growing my writing career, I began my days with daily journaling—stream-of-consciousness, typos and all—and I discovered three things fast:

- I believed charging more than $90/hour was "greedy."
- I had trouble carving out time to write my own books.
- My autoimmune flares spiked every time I said "yes" to a freelance project that wasn't the right fit for me.

As it turned out, naming the parasites made them evictable. When I identified these limiting beliefs, I changed everything. My rate hit $1,000/hour. My doctor said "remission." And I carved out enough time to write my own books, which began hitting bestseller lists.

Journaling isn't just a "feel better" exercise: it's an epiphany generator.

---

2. J. David Creswell and Emily K. Lindsay, "How Does Mindfulness Training Affect Health? A Mindfulness Stress Buffering Account," *Psychological Bulletin* 144, no. 4 (2018): 692–730, accessed 2025, https://www.ncbi.nlm.nih.gov/pmc/articles/PMC6220635/

How Meditation Moved Me From Chaotic Party Girl to Happy Yogi

In 2019 during my peak chaos and party girl era, I began my 200-hour yoga teacher training. I wasn't sure what to expect, but the most surprising part about showing up in the studio every Sunday for hours was how the regular meditation sessions began to shift something in me.

I would routinely spend Saturday night out late dancing to indie pop hits in a club with friends, and would stumble into morning yoga training hungover with big sunglasses, a venti caramel macchiato, and a pounding headache. However, the calming meditation on the wood floor of the West Los Angeles studio began to tickle a part of my brain that began asking questions.

A year and change later, I gave up alcohol forever, and closed the book on the chaos that had kept me company for so long when I lived in Los Angeles. I credit my yoga teacher training not only for the lifestyle changes that made me healthier and happier, but also for a neural renovation.

Since then, meditation unlocked my creativity and helped me hit writing goals I could only have dreamt of back in 2019 when my anxiety was on a hair trigger. The life I have today is thanks to the nervous system regulation practices I developed in my yoga teacher training.

Meditation is a lot more widespread in this day and age (I'm sure you've seen advertisements for the zillion meditation apps) so you're probably familiar with the laundry list of benefits of a consistent practice. If not, I'll highlight a 2024 review that logged measurable increases in cortical thickness and reduced amygdala reactivity after consistent meditation practice.[3] Translation: a regular meditation

---

3. Ying-Ying Zhou et al., "Digital Detox: Disconnecting for Mental Health and Wellbeing," *International Journal of Environmental Research and Public Health* 21, no. 8 (2024): 1132, accessed 2025, https://www.ncbi.nlm.nih.gov/pmc/articles/PMC11591838/

practice actively changes your brain, ensuring sharper thinking and less panic in the face of stressors.

There's a reason meditation shows up across spiritual traditions, creative disciplines, and even performance psychology. It helps you be present so you can break negative patterns. When you're constantly operating from fight-or-flight, your work suffers. Your thinking narrows. Your nervous system goes into defense mode. But when you meditate, you create space where new ideas, better strategies, and actual insight can emerge.

Meditation is one of the fastest, most effective ways I know to reset your brain, reconnect with your direction, and craft a clearer path to your ideal life. Not just in writing, but in how you move through your day.

The Ideal Day Drill: Write Your Future, Then Move In

The first time I tried the Ideal Day Drill, I was in Florence, Italy, in 2021.

I was deep in burnout. My autoimmune symptoms were flaring, my writing business was still a wild animal in what it demanded from me with too many clients and not enough time, and even though I had a lot going for me on paper, my body and my mind were fraying at the edges.

It was the last gasp of summer in Italy, and Kyle and I had checked into a hotel/co-working space that felt like a temporary haven: open-air lounges, a rooftop pool and gym that overlooked the ancient city, and a courtyard perfect for decompressing.

We were sitting outside in the courtyard, eating ciabatta sandwiches that were dotted with truffle sauce. They were the kind of sandwiches that made your eyes roll back into your head after every bite. It was a little slice of umami heaven even as I felt emotionally fried and overwhelmed by everything I was up to in my work life.

Kyle turned to me and asked, "What do you want your ideal day to look like?"

I didn't have an answer at first.

But I started describing it anyway: I want to wake up without an alarm. I want to write books for myself, not just for clients. I want to live a no-deadline life. I want the flexibility to work from anywhere, but also the grounding of a beautiful home base. I want to earn enough not just to live, but to also invest in my own work. I want space for creativity, health, stillness.

Kyle nodded. "Write that down."

So we did. Side by side with our notebooks in our laps, we wrote out what our perfect days looked like. We wrote and talked from the time that sunlight hit our faces to the moment we closed our laptops and wandered the cobblestone streets lit by glowing street lamps in search of some Florentine sourdough pizza for dinner.

After crafting my ideal day, I didn't think about it again. I was whisked back into my whirlwind of experimentation and growth. But somewhere deep in my mind, the concepts around my ideal day were burrowing into my vision for the future.

Fast forward to this past spring of 2025. After a week wandering Copenhagen, I flew back to Florence. Same streets. Same sandwich. But this time, I was returning as someone new. Someone who'd built the vision I'd had for myself nearly four years earlier.

After a few days retracing my steps in Florence, I made my way to the Tuscan countryside for a writing retreat led by bestselling author Emma Gannon. We stayed in a hundred-year-old farmhouse on an organic family-run farm. There were olive trees, fresh honey on the breakfast table, and long walks between writing sessions.

One morning, we gathered outside at a wrought-iron table under a blooming trellis. Wildflowers nodded in the breeze. The air smelled like lavender and wood smoke.

Emma asked us to do an exercise: write out your ideal day.

I recognized it instantly.

This time, when I put pen to paper, I was stunned. Every item I listed in 2021 had come true. My life was the page I had once imagined.

No alarm clock. No rushed deadlines. Time to write books that mattered to me. A flexible schedule that allowed me to prioritize my health. A home base in an exciting city. The freedom to hop on a plane when I needed beauty, newness, inspiration.

The ideal day I wrote down back when I first visited Italy was not aspirational anymore. It was all around me.

This is the power of the ideal day drill: it creates internal frameworks that change our external surroundings.

The mind doesn't always know what it wants until you walk it through every moment.

But there's a catch: specificity.

The more specific you are, the more your subconscious starts to work toward that outcome. Back in 2021, I had written timestamps for my ideal day. Mood notes, how my morning tea would taste. When I'd check emails (or not). That specificity built momentum. The details anchored my brain to possibility.

I designed that life.

And then I walked into it.

So here's your invitation: write down your ideal day. Then use this book to make it real.

Mental Models: Upgrade Your Mind's Operating System

Mental models are the core code of your internal operating system. They're how you parse reality, how you price yourself, and how you decide what kind of life is possible.

Language calibrates pricing, as well as how the world treats you. So let's revisit how you describe what you do, both to yourself and to others.

It's not "here's what I charge." It's "Here is the investment required to bring your book to life."

It's not "I'm a freelance writer." It's "I'm a luxury memoir ghostwriter."

Those shifts aren't cosmetic. They reframe value. They reposition power.

When I started describing my services in specific, high-conviction terms, something wild happened: people believed me. The language taught them how to treat me. It taught me how to treat myself. Clients stopped negotiating and just started paying invoices.

If you want to build a luxury brand, start with luxury language. Your copy, your pitch decks, and your onboarding flow all need to feel like a seamless extension of the rates you want to command. If your services sound cheap, don't be surprised when people ask for cheap prices.

Another operating system patch? Let's visit the concept I like to call *The Lens of 10x*.

In June 2023, I hadn't made a single dollar with my paid newsletter. I was still testing. Still proving. Then, I made a public declaration: I was going to scale my paid newsletter to $96,000/year.

It was audacious. Borderline laughable. That's the point.

The goal was $96,000 away from where I stood. But I set the target. I showed up. I published *every single week*. I focused on value. I built systems. I made noise. I delivered.

As of July 2025, I hit my goal, and then some: my paid newsletter has crossed over $100,000 in annual recurring revenue. The crazy high number was now my reality.

You need a goal so big it scares you into a new operating mode. You need a number or a milestone that demands new thoughts, new inputs, new strategies. Otherwise, you'll coast inside a comfort zone disguised as pragmatism.

Playing too small is far more dangerous than failing big. Because small goals don't stretch you. They don't magnetize support. They don't rewire your ambition.

Henry Ford's famous quote rings true here: "If you believe you can or can't, you're right." Because just like the power of positive self-talk, negative self-talk also has the ability to derail your goals. Your identity is shaped by the conversations you have with yourself.

If you want to be the kind of writer who earns $1,000,000/year, you have to start speaking like them, pitching like them, writing like them, and protecting your time like them. Self-talk is not just a nice-to-have habit. It's a settings panel.

Start telling yourself the truth you want to step into:

"I'm a bestselling author."

"I'm a luxury ghostwriter."

"I run a publishing studio, not a content shop."

"I'm a seven-figure writer, and I do what I love every day."

Your brain listens. So does your audience. So do your clients.

Upgrade your internal labels and the external world has no choice but to catch up.

Mindset in Action: How a Quote Became Six Figures

When my hourly ceiling was $90/hour I told myself it was practical—that clients wouldn't pay more. The truth: I felt like a freshman crashing a graduate seminar. My posture on Zoom curved inward, my voice pitched apologetic, and clients sensed it before we ever reached numbers. Imposter syndrome was written all over my presence.

Then I rewired my self-image. Vision board numbers turned into daily affirmations. Journaling surfaced the belief that "greedy" people charge four digits per hour. I deleted that story, replaced it with *luxury writers set market rates.*

After I replaced my identity, an international client asked me for a quote on a memoir.

My old brain panicked.

My new one said: "My rate is $1,000/hour."

Silence.

Then: "Send the invoice."

Next client? Bigger scope. Higher quote. Another yes.

Nothing in my portfolio changed. Just the story I told myself.

This entire book is built on that shift.

Ritual Stack: Your Daily Sequence

Let me be honest: I don't do rigid routines. I never have. One of the non-negotiables in my ideal life is flexibility.

I don't wake up at 5 a.m. on a regular basis. I don't follow a color-coded hourly planner. What I do follow is intention.

I use a modular schedule—a weekly dashboard where I track what actually matters: how many times I want to hit 10,000 steps, how often I want to go to yoga, how many deep work blocks I'm committing to. That dashboard keeps me grounded without turning my life into a checklist.

But, early on, when I was first exiting the full-time grind and learning how to live like a truly free writer, I needed something more structured. A container. A ritual reset. A way to rewire my nervous system and build habits that matched the life I was designing.

So if you're still building your version of freedom or if you're transitioning out of the 9-to-5 mindset, here's the foundational stack that kept me sane, productive, and in flow:

1. Mindful Wake-Up. Start your day without tech. No phone on your nightstand. Keep it in another room if you can. Wake up slowly. Three deep breaths. Stretch. Hydrate. Let your body arrive before the world does. If you're a parent or someone who doesn't have the luxury of a mindful wake-up, then find another pocket of your day to place this mindful moment.

2. Journal. Grab a notebook and pour. Stream-of-consciousness, no editing. Aim for three to four pages—or set a timer for ten to fifteen minutes. This is your mental detox, your subconscious debug log. Let it be messy. Let it be honest.

3. Meditate. Fifteen minutes. Sit with your breath. Or try a guided visualization. This is your first meditation session of the day (yes, I recommend two meditation sessions per day!) Ground your nervous system. Sharpen your awareness. Return to yourself before the distractions start.

4. Move Your Body. Strength training. A workout class. A brisk 30-minute walk. Whatever gets your blood flowing and energy unlocked. The goal isn't sweat for sweat's sake, it's kinetic clarity. Movement unblocks mental momentum. So many famous authors credit walking as their go-to for beating writer's block.

5. Eat a Real Breakfast. Ideally, protein-rich and whole foods. Something that fuels your brain and stabilizes your energy. Fuel for the kind of execution you want in your day.

6. Vision Board Review. Look at your vision board—the one on your phone, your desktop wallpaper, or your wall. Don't just glance. Feel it. Speak one affirmation aloud. One of my favorites? *I don't chase, I attract. The good that belongs to me will simply find me.*

7. First Deep Work Block. No text messages. No inbox. No task switching. Just focused, meaningful work that moves your goals forward or your revenue higher. I like to theme my days: deep work on some, admin on others. Either way, start the day in alignment with what matters most.

There's no magic bullet routine that works for everyone.

Some people swear by a strict 5 a.m. miracle morning. That's not me. Some people repeat the same ritual sequence every single day. That's not me either.

You have to figure out what actually supports you. Your body. Your brain. Your lifestyle. Your responsibilities.

But here's what is universal: consistency beats complexity.

So build your own ritual stack. Create a checklist of habits your ideal self does most days. Track it weekly. And let that checklist be a mirror: *What would the happy, healthy, seven-figure version of me do today?* Then do it. Does waking up early set up your best life? Great, set a bedtime alarm so you can wind down earlier and get more sleep and wake up refreshed. It's up to you to set yourself up for success in whatever way that looks like for you.

This is the cheat code. You don't need a perfect morning routine. You need consistent action tied to your next identity.

Lofty goals alone won't save you.

But habits will change your life.

From Tarot Cards to Chakras: Embodying Life in Color

In Copenhagen, I did tarot pulls in between boat tours and smørrebrød tasting. In Kyoto, I did yoga nearly every day during my month-long visit to reset my nervous system. In Tuscany, I visited an 80-year-old energy healer who told me my throat chakra was blocked by an ancestral ghost.

No matter if I'm traveling or at home, I've identified the types of experiences that expand my view of what it means to be human. In finding ways to sift through my inner world, I improved my outer world.

As writers, that rich inner world is key to honing our creativity and keeping our minds sharp. But maybe you're allergic to incense. That's fine: keep what resonates. Discard the rest.

However, the thing I've discovered most during my years of traveling as a digital nomad? Extraordinary outcomes require non-ordinary inputs.

What does this look like for you? Find an openness to new experiences and new ways of living. You don't need to travel the world or become a monk to unlock something more special, but the concept of "garbage in, garbage out" applies here if the only way you're experiencing life is through a phone screen.

Power Move: Design the Day, Build the Board

For this Power Move, combine the Ideal Day Drill with a vision board that brings it to life.

First, write out your perfect Tuesday in your life in great detail. Be specific: what are you wearing? What do you talk about with your partner over breakfast? What are the deposits that hit your bank accounts? Who calls you to congratulate and support you?

Then, image hunt like your future depends on it.

Search image websites. Screenshot hotels and your future home. Paste in the exact espresso machine, the gym, the custom-built desk. Save it as your wallpaper on your devices, or even print it out and hang it somewhere.

This is not a dream.

It's a dress rehearsal for reality.

Amy's Field Notes: Your New Identity Starts Now

A few years ago, I was running around Buenos Aires with a pack of international nomads, watching tango dancers twirl under neon streetlamps. The city had a pulse. Palermo felt like a storybook with pastel walls, bookstores on every block, and the kind of cafés where creative people actually made things instead of just sipping cortados while doomscrolling.

But I wasn't making anything.

At least, not for myself.

When new friends asked what I was working on, I rattled off ghostwriting projects and nonfiction business plans. But the truth? I felt a bit hollow. I had built a lucrative writing career, but somewhere along the way, I'd stopped feeding the part of me that wrote for joy. For curiosity. For the thrill of invention.

I told myself I didn't have time to write fiction with everything going on, even though I felt a pang of loss at my past endeavors in writing fiction for other mediums.

Then, one night after a dinner at a tapas bar where conversation revolved around what we wanted for the future, the answer hit me: writing fiction wasn't a luxury. It was part of my DNA.

That night, I had a dream.

The next morning, I went to my usual sunny coffeeshop around the corner, ordered a flat white, a Pão de Queijo, and opened my laptop and typed the words: *Violet Chase was not in the mood to solve a murder.*

I didn't know who she was yet, but I wanted to. She was a digital nomad, bouncing between coworking spaces and crime scenes, investigating a suspicious string of deaths inside the tight-knit remote work world. She became the main character of my first short story collection I eventually titled *The Nomad Detective.*

It scared the hell out of me. I hadn't published fiction in years. The voice in my head whispered: *You're rusty. You're out of practice. Who do you think you are?*

But I ignored the voice and kept going. I wrote in cafés in

Argentina. On trains in Japan. At a Blue Bottle in Kyoto, where the café had big, wood-paneled windows and I watched people bike past in crisp linen. I wrote slow. I wrote messy. I wrote scared.

And eventually, I hit publish.

That little book didn't make headlines. But it did something better: it made me brave again. Other nomads started messaging me. A woman in Lisbon said she'd cried reading one of Violet's monologues. A friend in Seoul asked when the next one was coming out. A podcast host told me *The Nomad Detective* cracked something open in her.

That book led to me writing my first romantasy novel, *The Ash Trials*, which led to an entirely new chapter of my author career.

But more importantly: it led me back to myself.

And it all started because I decided to pretend.

Not fake. Not force. *Pretend.*

There's this weird truth about the human brain: to fall asleep, you have to pretend you're asleep. That's the trick. You breathe like a sleeper. You lay still like a sleeper. You fall asleep through the act of pretending.

Same with identity.

You want to become a bestselling author? Pretend you already are. Sit down and write the scene. Build the vision board. Own the café window seat and show up with your damn laptop and your dreams in tow. The more you live like the person you want to be, the faster your reality catches up.

Pretending is about rehearsal. You're not faking it. You're building the muscle memory of a future truth.

And one day, when someone asks what you do, you won't flinch. You'll say it out loud. "I'm a fiction author. I write books I want to read. I move people with words."

Because you practiced that line until it was no longer fiction.

It was a fact.

4

FOCUS AS YOUR SECRET WEAPON

W e live in a culture engineered to fracture your attention. Social media monetizes your distraction. Your inbox is a war zone. Your to-do list is probably a graveyard of half-finished priorities competing for the same sliver of bandwidth. If you're working a 9-to-5 while building your dream career in the margins, you know the pressure of trying to fit your entire life into evenings and weekends.

That was me. I believed I could do it all if I just caffeinated harder. That focus was something optional, something for minimalists or those with an abundance of free time. But I was wrong.

In a world that wants you distracted, choosing to focus is an act of true power.

The Midnight-Oil Mirage

In your twenties, you run on the midnight oil—that late-night fuel that lets you bang out ten pages at 2 a.m., then show up fresh-faced to your day job five hours later. Energy feels infinite, so you don't have to prioritize it.

But midnight oil is a non-renewable resource.

Around your late twenties—sooner if you've been stress-sprinting—you notice the tank doesn't refill. You try to push through, but the well coughs up sand. You say things like, "I used to party until dawn, ace a final, and rewrite a pilot all in the same week."

The empty well of energy doesn't care about what you "used" to do.

Kyle connected the idea of burning the midnight oil to why working for gatekeepers in your twenties can be so sinister.

"Who are you really burning that precious midnight oil for? Yourself? Or are you burning your high energy years for companies and institutions that don't care for you?" Kyle mused during a road trip we took around the United States with our friends. Long car rides led to conversations breaking down where we'd been and what had been taken from us.

What's being taken from *you*.

So what happens when your natural supply of energy and youthful go-go-go mentality starts to dwindle? The midnight oil is replaced with focus. Not the multitasking, tab-hoarding kind. The weaponized kind—the kind that turns your effort into impact.

Lamp vs. Laser

Greg McKeown's excellent book *Essentialism* nails the metaphor of how we spend our energy.

Picture two circles, each fed by the same amount of energy.

The first shoots a dozen arrows in every direction. It's a lamp, illuminating everything but igniting nothing.

The second shoots one concentrated beam. A laser. Because the light is focused, it can burn through steel. The lamp, on the other hand, doesn't stand a chance against a piece of sheet metal.

Hollywood and traditional systems train writers to stay in lamp mode. "Keep five scripts going," the agents say. "Keep multiple irons in the fire." Translation: diffused energy makes you docile and conveniently controllable. No wonder so many talented writers spend a decade orbiting good ideas that never escape gravity.

I attempted to keep up with the multiplying demands of the industry. One pilot here, three features there, freelance copy on the side. Progress everywhere. Momentum nowhere.

Then I picked my targets. On the creative side? My romantasy novel *The Ash Trials*. I wrote it start to finish in four months. It got more praise than scripts I'd tinkered with for years. On the writing business side? I raised my freelance writing rates from $90/hour to $1,000/hour during the five years I poured real focus into growing my ghostwriting services.

When I stopped diffusing my energy and started directing it, things started breaking through.

Discovery Mode vs. Execution Mode

So what does focus *actually* look like? It doesn't mean permanent tunnel vision. Focus has seasons.

Here are the two modes I believe you should intentionally shift between:

1. **Discovery Mode** is lamp time. You explore, research, brainstorm, chase rabbit holes, soak up inspiration. The goal is curiosity and possibility. Discovery Mode is great for trying out different types of freelance writing specialties to see what you enjoy better. Or it may be great for playing around with a new project like a paid newsletter to see where your interests lead you. Discovery Mode helps you see what's possible before you commit to a project or a path. The mistake most writers make is staying in *Discovery Mode* too long, or trying to multitask both modes at once.

2. **Execution Mode** is laser time. You pick the one project that hits your gut like a tuning fork and shut down everything else. Calendar blocks. App blockers. Your personal green light to go all in. Sometimes writers struggle with Execution Mode because this is where the limiting belief of "writer's block" loves to try and shut you down and force you back in Discovery Mode. Writer's block isn't real: it's just a

codename for a weak muscle of resiliency you need to build up over time by truly committing your entire focus and dedication to the demands of Execution Mode. Don't let task-switching, distractions, or a negative internal monologue pull you off course.

When it's time to execute, treat the transition like a launch sequence: start in Discovery Mode, and then once you're ready to light up the sky with your creativity, move into Execution Mode. Declare it publicly. Set a timeline. Make it hard to back out. Discovery fuels creativity, but execution delivers results.

Flow: The Furnace That Shapes Steel

I became a writer because I loved the feeling of my fingers flying across the keyboard as words appeared on the page. Hours would go by and I would forget to eat as I was completely consumed by the act of writing.

Psychologist Mihaly Csikszentmihalyi called it flow—that state where hours vanish and the writing feels channeled instead of typed. That's the "writer's high" of the flow state I'm always chasing. Similar to a runner's high, it takes effort and skill to attain, but it's euphoric all the same.

However, flow requires depth. Splintered attention murders it.

As James Clear, author of the must-read book *Atomic Habits* reminds us: unfinished projects do *not* compound. Every half-written draft resets your momentum. Every abandoned project or return to Discovery Mode because you couldn't finish something only sets you back further.

On the other hand, finished work compounds twice: once in revenue, and again in reputation.

This is why focus is a superpower. It allows you to actually complete the projects you say you want to do, and turns "one day" into today.

Fear: The Quiet Thief of Focus

Why do we cling to half-written everything? Why do we split our focus between projects or even industries?

Fear.

Fear of betting wrong. Of wasting time. Of failing in public.

I didn't go all in on full-time freelancing for years because mentors told me there was a ceiling for what I could make and accomplish as a freelance writer on my own. Then the pandemic shut down my writers' room. I went all in on freelancing—and my income tripled.

The ceiling was fake. My scattered focus had kept it intact.

Focus feels risky because it makes failure visible. But diffusion is the bigger risk because it guarantees mediocrity.

The Laser Protocol

Before we dive in, let's set the stage. You don't need to be a Luddite or throw your phone in a lake. But you do need a system.

When my freelance writing business first started to really take off in 2020, I was still treating it like a side project squeezed between Hollywood writers' rooms and odd deadlines. I hadn't yet allowed myself to go all in. My days were a patchwork of client calls, half-finished drafts, and frantic espresso runs. I told myself I was "working" but what I was really doing was trying to sprint across a minefield of distractions. It was clear in the results: my inbox overflowed, my file system was chaos, my body was dehydrated, and my brain was "twired," or Kyle's word for that wired-but-tired state you hit after mainlining caffeine at 11 p.m. without moving the needle on anything meaningful.

Kyle had seen this before. Back then we were just friends, not yet romantic partners, and he was already something of a Zen master of productivity. Pre-2020, we'd spend afternoons in boba tea shops where he'd sit, headphones in, quietly perfecting a single line of a script for hours while the world blurred around him. I'd work beside him and marvel at his discipline. He wasn't militant about it—he'd take breaks, chat with me and whoever else was writing nearby—but his focus was a kind of gravity. People stayed in orbit around it.

One day he came over to my apartment in Los Angeles to help me figure out why my days were collapsing under their own weight. I'd been bragging about how "busy" I was, but when he actually sat down at a makeshift desk next to mine and quietly observed, he saw the truth. My phone vibrated every minute. App pings and random calls poured in. Delivery people rang the doorbell. All my appliances were going at once—laundry tumbling, coffee pot gurgling—a chorus of distractions. Papers were stacked everywhere. I hadn't had a sip of water in hours. My email was a slot machine of unread subject lines, and my whiteboard was a graveyard of scribbled to-dos that never got crossed out.

After an hour, Kyle looked up from his laptop. "It's surprising how much you got done," he said, "but you rushed the whole way through." His point wasn't that I was lazy, it was that I was splintered. I had the bones of a system, but too much noise to let anything breathe.

Then he walked me through his minimalist productivity protocol. Turn off all notifications on every device except truly urgent calls or texts. Start the day with reflection and journaling, not inbox triage. Batch emails and calls in defined "admin" blocks. Protect deep work at all costs. Keep your workspace, desktop, and inbox clear to support a clear mind. He even bought me a "smart" water bottle that measured how much water I drank in a day, a gentle intervention to rehydrate my brain along with my calendar.

At first, it felt unnatural. My distractions had become a kind of comfort, and a way to avoid going all in on my own work. But as I followed his advice, my mental static started to fade. I realized my biggest problem wasn't time management. It was identity management. By treating my freelance writing like a side hustle instead of a full-time creative business, I'd allowed myself to stay scattered.

The Laser Protocol—my name for the system I've adapted from Kyle's productivity rules—was more than a list of hacks. For me, it was a reset button for my nervous system and my mindset. It forced me to decide: was I going to keep playing small, darting between other people's priorities, or was I ready to focus like a real business owner?

Today, I still use Kyle's protocol. My phone stays quiet. My mornings start slow. My workspace is a landing strip for ideas, not clutter. And yes, I drink my water. More importantly, I've learned that the discipline of focus is really the discipline of choosing yourself. You can't build a seven-figure writing career from the scraps of your attention. You have to carve out a block of uninterrupted, undiluted presence and move through it like a laser.

This is the heart of the Laser Protocol: the courage to give what you're working on your true focus. It's a way to build the conditions for your best work to emerge, and to teach your brain, day after day, that your dreams deserve your full attention.

Even if you don't have a Kyle in your life, you can still steal his digital makeover to get a focus-friendly approach to your work.

Here's how to flip from scattered to sharp:

1. **Energy Audit.** Track your peak creative hours for one week. Then, use a time-tracking tool to see how you're really spending your time. What's draining your energy reserves? What's being done at the wrong time? Then, protect your peak hours like they print money—because they do.

2. **Project Triage.** List every active idea you have. Circle one. Archive the rest in a "later" folder. Relief is instant. Focus on your top priority, and put everything else secondary.

3. **Time Blocking.** Block at least two hours of uninterrupted deep work. Thirty-minute scraps won't cut it—unless that's all you have access to, in which case just work with what you've got. However, if you have control over your schedule, try and build up to three to four hours of deep work per work day and see how your goals accelerate and your laser rips through all obstacles.

4. **Public Stakes.** Tell someone. Your group chat, your partner, your newsletter readers. Set up pre-orders on your book so you *have*

to upload your book files for a real deadline. External accountability focuses the beam.

5. Environment Engineering. Phone off. Tabs closed. Ritual helps signal to your brain: laser mode engaged.

6. Recovery Cycles. Move your body. Touch grass. Nap. Burned-out lasers melt themselves first.

7. Finish Relentlessly. Ship it and hit publish.

In my book *Six-Figure Freelance Writer,* I introduced you to the concept of "Admin Days" versus "Deep Work Days." I still stand behind this method where you place your heavy-lift creative sessions into three or four days per week and then corral the inbox, invoices, and calendar shuffling into the scraps that remain.

In this book, I'm expanding on that concept. In the past few years, I've also zoomed out to create the concept of "Growth Weeks" and "Maintenance Weeks."

Growth Weeks are pedal-to-the-metal: chapter sprints, launch prep, client marathons. These are the weeks you push for massive growth and progress.

Maintenance Weeks are the built-in pit stop: a little admin, a little reading, maybe a light writing warm-up, then an early clock-out so the brain can wander. These are the weeks you play hooky and book an 11 a.m. brunch with fellow creative friends with flexible schedules rather than grind it out at your desk.

I shoot for one Maintenance Week after every three or four Growth Weeks, tweaking the ratio for deadlines, travel, or hormonal cycles.

The payoff of finding the right balance of the gas pedal and the brake is guilt-free productivity that matches real-world energy rhythms and keeps the creative engine purring.

Power Move: The One-Project Pledge

Choose one creative project this month that you will move across the finish line. It can be a draft, a pitch, a landing page, a proposal, a script. Anything that matters.

Announce it. Write it down. Calendar the work sessions.

Then treat that project like it's the only thing standing between you and your next level, because it might be.

Amy's Field Notes: Finding Focus in Paris

My trip to Paris wasn't part of some master plan. It started with a last-minute decision to see my favorite band Glass Animals play live. That was the headline. But the real story unfolded quietly over croissants and cobblestone streets, antique flea markets, and late-night conversations.

It was November 2024, the tail end of a year that had taken me everywhere: Istanbul, Kyoto, Seoul, and beyond. A year of beauty and momentum. I had published *The Nomad Detective*, continued to grow my ghostwriting business, and was watching my Substack, Make Writing Your Job, start to take on a life of its own. New paid subscribers were rolling in daily, ping after ping like tiny confetti cannons on my phone. It was exciting, chaotic, a little surreal. This was all happening as we were living on the top floor of an apartment in Montmartre with a view of the Eiffel Tower out one window and Sacré-Cœur out the other. Paris unfolded below us like a map we had somehow earned the right to read.

Our mornings were slow. We'd walk down the street, stopping at a small store for these incredible sandwiches made from farm-fresh produce on homemade baguettes. We visited an expat friend at a café, meandered the Musée d'Orsay, and dipped into boutiques and bookstores with no agenda. But behind the wandering was something else: a sharpening.

On one particular morning, Kyle and I were walking to the *Marché aux Puces de la Porte de Vanves*, a local Paris flea market, heading to meet up with friends. As we crossed into that beautiful, chaotic maze of antique stalls, with gilded mirrors and old film posters stacked like playing cards, the conversation Kyle and I were having shifted. What do we want to focus on? What matters enough to warrant our full attention next year?

Kyle and I kept walking. And by the time we reached our friends, we had decided.

For the next twelve months, we'd grow Make Writing Your Job into something self-sustaining, a true community platform. I'd keep executing my highest-leverage client projects with care, but would be careful to not take on too much. Then, I'd make space to finish *The Ash Trials* before its February release. That was it. Three things. No more.

We didn't write it down that day. But we carved it into our reality.

And since then? That focus has held. With a few detours, of course. This is life, not a factory line, after all. However, our energy moved in the direction we pointed it after that conversation. The Substack became the flagship. A team formed around me. *The Ash Trials* debuted as my first romantasy novel. And now, as I write these pages, we're packing our bags for a month in China, knowing that our systems and our team will keep the engine running while we chase inspiration across time zones.

Sometimes I look back and laugh at my 2019 and early 2020 self. The scattered version of me who was "twired" all day, with my inbox overflowing and buried in "maybe" projects would have crumbled under the weight of what I'm doing now. She wanted to do everything all at once. But she didn't yet know that focus isn't a limitation. It's a spell. It conjures the future you actually want.

Focus is what gave me a business that runs with my values baked in. It's what gave me a paid newsletter and backlist of self-published books with a readership that grows while I sleep. It's what gave me the space to fall in love with fiction again. And to fall in love, full stop, with someone whose systems rewired not just my productivity but my belief in what's possible when you stop running from your own potential.

You don't need to go to Paris to make this shift. You don't need a partner to sit beside you and talk you through the chaos. (Though I do recommend both, if offered.) What you do need is the courage to name what you want and to give it the unbroken attention it deserves.

Because here's the truth: every year, I become someone new. And every version of me that I've loved most—the writer, the founder, the romantic, the student of wonder—all arrived because I bet on myself again. And again. And again.

Focus is just another word for commitment. And commitment is how dreams get made.

So make the list. Make the plan. Light the beam.

I'm cheering for you.

5

HATERS PROVE THE WORK MATTERS, SO KEEP TYPING

Backlash is your stamped receipt for boundary-pushing work. It means you struck a nerve. It means you're no longer creating from the safety of silence. When your work matters, it echoes and attracts both applause and opposition.

If you don't have haters, you're not saying anything new, or *true*. Because the truth pisses people off. That's just physics.

Before we continue, let me say that this isn't a call to manufacture controversy or slop together rage-bait just to stir the pot. That's cheap and forgettable. This is about owning the consequences of telling the truth as you see it, and continuing to create in full view of the fallout.

When your ideas challenge someone's worldview, their comfort, or their self-image, they lash out. It has nothing to do with you. It's their internal war, projected in your direction. You just happened to say the thing they've been trying not to admit to themselves.

If you doubt this, go read the one-star reviews for the books for any author you admire. Nobody gets out clean. Even your favorite book written by a beloved author has inspired a stranger to write an entire paragraph about how it ruined their afternoon and slap a one star onto it. Welcome to the arena.

Even the early drafts of this book drew blood. One beta reader dubbed me "Girl Boss Barbie," which honestly belongs on a t-shirt in my future merch line. A younger version of me might've spiraled over the 10-15% of negative feedback in the pile. But this time around, I screenshotted the messages from readers who called this their new writing business bible and I filtered the rest for what was actually useful. Some of the most disgruntled readers gave me the most actionable notes. But I wouldn't have found those insights if I hadn't been willing to sit with the sting long enough to hear the signal underneath the snark.

So here we are: this chapter is your training ground for staying bold even when the knives come out.

When Universal Approval Felt Like a Straightjacket

My darkest creative year was the one with the most applause. My bosses loved my work. Executives were thrilled that I would do free rewrites on scripts. I was a team player, a polite rewriter, a professional yes-woman. Everyone liked me.

And I hated my life.

I wasn't making anything of my own. I was taking notes, playing nice, rewriting scripts that weren't mine, working for free, and getting nowhere.

Then I tried something different.

I founded Kingdom of Pavement, a scrappy literary and performance collective in Los Angeles. We ran open mics, published poetry, and produced scripted podcast dramas. And for the first time in years, I felt electric.

And then came the backlash.

The more buzz we built, the more the sharks circled. Friends-turned-consultants tried to hijack budgets. Disgruntled collaborators issued legal threats. It was chaotic and messy and exhilarating (in retrospect).

The price of momentum is a target on your back. But it was a price I was willing to pay to enter the arena, tell stories, and take bold creative risks. Here's something to remember when you're wading through the haters: the people who are actually successful and finding happiness? They're never going to waste time trying to cut you down. It's only the people who feel threatened by you in some way who will go out of their way to try and hurt you.

Welcome to Chapter Five.

The Math of Outrage

Here's how the physics of attention works:

1. Attention is finite.
2. Creative risk attracts attention, both good and bad.
3. When your work carries real stakes, it creates polarity.
   And polarity is how you break through.

If everyone agrees with you, you've probably made something forgettable. Because "playing it safe" kills resonance. The truth is sharp. It scrapes. It stings. And that sting is what makes it memorable.

Criticism is the tax you pay for leaving the comfort zone. The critics live in the cheap seats. The creators are in the arena, bleeding under the lights.

In a famous speech given by Teddy Roosevelt in 1910, he states:

"It is not the critic who counts; not the man who points out how the strong man stumbles, or where the doer of deeds could have done them better. The credit belongs to the man who is actually in the arena, whose face is marred by dust and sweat and blood; who strives valiantly; who errs, who comes short again and again, because there is no effort without error and shortcoming; but who does actually strive to do the deeds; who knows great enthusiasms, the great devotions; who spends himself in a worthy cause; who at the best knows in the end the triumph of high achievement, and who at the worst, if he fails, at least fails while daring greatly, so that his place shall never be with those cold and timid souls who neither know victory nor defeat."

Critics are loud because they're building nothing, and they're definitely *not* daring greatly. That's what makes a heckler. They comment on the play-by-play without ever stepping on stage. And yes, some criticism is insightful, important, and necessary. But the people who tear you down for sport? They're allergic to courage.

Sometimes your loudest naysayers won't be strangers. They'll be so-called friends who see you succeeding and let a green-eyed monster grow within them. Stay far away from fake friends who don't want the best for you, and be brave enough to forge ahead to find the people who will support the best evolution of your life. And no matter what? Always keep typing.

Case Study: "Getting Paid $50,000 to Write a Memoir is Impossible."

Last year, I had a client offer me $50,000 for a memoir ghostwriting project. That was way below my current rates at the time, so I shared the opportunity with my writing job board at MakeWritingYourJob.com.

An editor of another writing newsletter saw the job. The editor emailed me, convinced the job couldn't be real.

"No one pays $50,000 for a memoir," she said. "That's impossibly high."

I had proof, of course, but it wasn't worth my time to share with her. But here's the punchline: one of my newsletter readers applied to the open memoir job, got hired, and emailed me a thank-you note. It was a win for the writer who believed they could charge what some people get paid in a *year* to ghostwrite a memoir for an exciting client. This is one of the many reasons I love seeing writers win on my writing job board and beyond.

Here's the irony of this whole situation: if I'd shared my actual rates for what expert writers like myself get paid for memoirs, that editor would've blown a gasket.

Backlash is often just other people's limiting beliefs breaking under the weight of your reality. People will try to take shots at your self-worth to soothe their own insecurities. Just know that they're not talking to you when they try to cut you down: they're talking to themselves and trying to quiet their own fears.

When critics come for you, ask: *Did this widen my reach? Did it sharpen my tribe or my resolve?* If yes, you've already been paid in full.

Mindsets That Bulletproof Your Momentum

You're going to need thicker skin. Not to numb yourself, but to stay in motion when the noise gets loud.

Here's what to remember:

- **Critics fade. Work endures.** One-star reviews might be loud today, but libraries last centuries.
- **Haters show up once you rise.** They're just a side effect of altitude.
- **You can't reason with people committed to misunderstanding you.** Let them rant. They're not your audience, not your tribe.
- **Backlash is data, not destiny.** The hot zones of critique are often where your next breakthrough lives—either in listening to it, or in heading in the exact opposite direction.

Tactical Shields for the Modern Creator

When you set out to enter the arena, you have to put on your proverbial armor.

Here's how to stay protected without diluting yourself:

- **The Comment Detox Diet.** Limit time spent reading the comments. I read and respond to comments in certain windows of time. The rest of the time? Comments stay closed. You're not a suggestion box.
- **The Receipts Folder.** Screenshot praise, client wins, sales notifications. On troll days, scroll your highlight reel.

- **The Feedback Fence.** Only trusted peers get to weigh in. Internet randos are not on the editorial board.
- **The Hype Squad.** Keep close a small group of fellow creators, writers, and entrepreneurs who get it. Trade courage when yours runs low.
- **The Real World Reminder.** Most haters would never say what they leave in comments to your face in real life. If the pressure gets intense, log off and spend more time away from screens to instantly lower the volume.

The goal isn't to build walls so high no one can reach you, it's to set the terms for how you'll show up. Protect your energy. Choose your battles, curate your inputs, and invest in the people and practices that keep you clear-eyed and unshakable. That's how you keep creating at your sharpest, no matter what the internet trolls throw at you.

Why Playing It Safe Is the Real Risk

Look at the show *Survivor,* where strangers are stranded on deserted islands and forced to survive. Early seasons were chaos and strategy and unforgettable meltdowns between bold moves. Now it's TED Talks about integrity between rice rations. Ratings slip, social feeds shrug, and a once-feral show feels domesticated.

Your writing risks the same fate.

Safe means invisible. If your words offend no one, they will move no one. Polished neutrality does not change lives, or sell books.

Again, don't just be inflammatory for the sake of it, just say what's real and true and drop the mic.

Your 5-Step Hater-Resistant Action Plan

Haters are baked into the recipe of visibility. Once you publish with clarity and consistency, some people will clap, some will copy, and some will come unglued. Let them do whatever they need to do.

Below is your five-step blueprint for building a resilience engine even in the presence of haters:

1. Consistently Ship Bold Work. Not rage bait, but truth bait. The things you've hesitated to say, the stories you've buried under "maybe later," the essays that feel risky because they're raw—those are your signal flares. Set them loose. Let them find your true tribe.

2. Log Reactions: Measure Buzz, Not Feelings. Your feelings aren't data. Your metrics are. Keep a digital note or dashboard to track shares and replies. Use these to guide future decisions, not the knot in your stomach after one snarky comment.

3. Double Down on the Hot Zones. If a post ruffled feathers and got bookmarked fifty times? That's a hit. Distinguish between high-engagement provocation and low-value outrage. Spirited discourse is useful. Drive-by trollage? Ignore and forget. Courage without discernment burns out fast.

4. Celebrate the First Public Drag. You got called delusional, arrogant, or cringe? Congratulations, you're in the arena now. Smile at the temper tantrum, toast with espresso, and file it in your "Proof of Life" folder. Bonus points if it arrives with a bump in subscribers. Your success just gave someone an identity crisis. Cheers to that.

5. Keep Typing. Volume drowns hecklers. Flood the feed with books, essays, paid newsletters, courses—whatever lives in your creative pipeline. Let your work be so loud, so prolific, so wildly resonant that the critics end up buried under your royalty dashboard and "invoice paid" notifications. Let them whisper while you skip your way to the bank.

The haters are part of the journey. Welcome them. Smile. Offer them front-row seats to your rise—because you've got the keyboard, the receipts, and this book full of secrets on how to build your empire. Breezing past your haters and their ill will is just the warm-up act.

Final Word: Critics Die Anonymous, Creators Echo for Centuries

Michelangelo caught heat from the Church for filling *The Last Judgment* with muscle-packed, fully nude saints. Emily Dickinson was called eccentric. Beethoven was ridiculed for his wild compositions, then wrote a symphony no one could ignore, even after he went deaf.

Their critics? Forgotten. Their art? Canon and core to the syllabus we learn from today.

So when the hecklers circle, smile. You've entered the arena where echoes outlive noise.

Write the next thing.

Wave goodbye to your haters.

Publish anyway.

History has a long memory—and a short tolerance for cowards.

Power Move: Publish a Lightning Rod

This week, share one piece of writing that makes you a little scared to share—in a good way.

That blog post you've been editing for months. That essay that goes a little too hard. That truth you've tiptoed around.

Post it. Track what happens. Then post again.

Criticism means you're in motion. Keep moving.

Amy's Field Notes: The $750/Hour Rate and the Client Who Couldn't Handle It

It was a chaotic kind of magic in that stretch of time in Manhattan after *Six-Figure Freelance Writer* had dropped.

I was sprinting from podcast interviews to client calls to a storytelling panel where I half-jogged offstage just to make it back in time for a Zoom meeting. Our brownstone had high ceilings and a tiny balcony overlooking a garden that might as well have been a mirage. I saw it through the window more than I actually stepped outside. I was drowning in projects. Ghostwriting two memoirs. Copywriting on contract. Editing someone's 80,000-word book into something that would more accurately capture their story.

At $350/hour, I was fully booked and deeply underwater.

I picked up *$100M Offers* by Alex Hormozi sometime around midnight one night, unable to sleep. Hormozi said if you're in a market flooded with other freelancers, be the one charging *three times* more than anyone else. That idea hit me like a lightning bolt, or more accurately, like an electric cattle prod to the brain of someone who hadn't taken a real day off in two months.

So I made the jump.

$750/hour. No discount. No explanation. No "let me justify this to you with a 17-paragraph email." Just a number. Take it or leave it.

That same week, I got a message from a potential client on a freelance platform.

"Hey," he wrote, "I think there's a typo in your rate. You added an extra zero. It should be $75."

I was sitting on the couch, laptop perched on my knees, the last of my oat milk matcha next to me. I read the message twice. Maybe three times. Not because I was shocked, but because I could already feel the heat of the response forming, and I wanted to be sure I kept it cool.

"Nope," I wrote back. "My rate is $750/hour. If that's within your budget, I'd be happy to talk further."

I didn't tell him about the waitlist of memoir clients. Or the fact that I'd just turned down a five-figure project because I physically didn't have time to take it on. Or the panel talk, or the inbox overflow, or the ghostwriting deadlines breathing down my neck. I didn't explain that this was the only way to buy back even an hour of my life.

Because you don't owe anyone your justification. Especially not the guy who follows up with a message so petty and gendered and venomous it's not even worth printing here.

That's the thing about haters: they don't actually hate *you*. They hate what you represent. They hate the fact that you had the audacity to name your value out loud. To ask for more than they think you deserve. To raise your rate instead of your blood pressure.

But the best part?

An hour later, a different client booked me at $750/hour without blinking, and didn't even ask to hop on a call. This new client just sent over the contract and paid the invoice. No call. No pushback. No "Are you sure?" Just: "Great. Looking forward to working together."

Those two clients saw the same skill set, same writer, same materials. One person sees arrogance. The other sees expertise.

Don't lower your prices to accommodate someone's limited imagination.

Keep typing.

6

THE ART OF GETTING PAID

Every time I meet a suffering-for-the-art purist, they blame the usual cartoon villains: capitalism, gatekeepers, whatever headline is trending on social media. Meanwhile their brush is dry because they refuse to hit publish and monetize.

Newsflash: artists have been paid handsomely for millennia. The proof is everywhere once you stop doom-scrolling.

This chapter is here to break that spell. Because starving is not a requirement of the job. It's propaganda—one that defies how artists were seen in the past. Let's rewind.

Act I: Patronage: Renaissance Checks That Would Make Your Payroll App Blush

The original freelance economy? The Church.

Back in the Renaissance, religious institutions were the biggest arts funders on Earth. They didn't just pray for inspiration, they *paid* for it. Patronage was their payroll system. You had a talent, they had a vault. Boom: contract. Don't believe me? Book a flight to Europe and take one look at the stained glass and insane architecture. Patronage is responsible for what tourists pay the big bucks to see even now.

Even Shakespeare had stakeholder status. Will wasn't some quill-in-mouth romantic scraping by on sonnets. He was a part-owner of the Globe Theatre. That stake meant royalties, revenue shares, and steady payouts every time a groundling bought a ticket. Historians estimate he earned around £200 a year from his shares alone—solid six-figure territory today—on top of a cut from every sold-out show.[1] [2] [OBJ] [OBJ]

Lesson from the Renaissance: patronage is partnership. Find one powerful believer and you leapfrog the rent spiral.

Today's patrons are startups, solo founders, venture-backed CEOs, media companies, newsletter subscribers. They don't wear robes or carry scepters, but they do hire you. And we'll talk more about how to position yourself to land high-level patrons (especially as a ghostwriter) in a future chapter.

For now, remember: patrons are *not* traditional gatekeepers. They're clients. You have the power in these relationships unlike anything you've likely experienced with gatekeepers who remove your ability to truly negotiate. Don't believe me? We'll talk more about this in Part Two.

Act II: Print Revolutions: Serialization and the First Author-Influencers

The Industrial Age was transformed by a new invention: the printing press. With it came newspapers, magazines, and the rise of authors who could earn per installment.

Charles Dickens was paid by the cliffhanger. Dickens negotiated fat fees for serialized novels like *The Pickwick Papers*, then doubled up

---

1. Shakespeare Birthplace Trust, "How Much Was Shakespeare Worth?" *Let's Talk Shakespeare Podcast*, accessed 2025, https://www.shakespeare.org.uk/explore-shakespeare/podcasts/lets-talk-shakespeare/how-much-was-shakespeare-worth/

2. Biography.com Editors, "How Wealthy Was William Shakespeare?" *Biography.com*, accessed 2025, https://www.biography.com/authors-writers/a64501905/william-shakespeare-wealth.

with sold-out reading tours across America.[3] Adjusted for today, the guy banked millions and bought the kind of real estate English nobles envy.[4]

Harriet Beecher Stowe, Arthur Conan Doyle, and Alexandre Dumas all sold work piece-by-piece to periodicals, collecting checks every week instead of waiting for a hardcover payout. They didn't wait for book deals. They monetized as they wrote.

Even in today's age, serialization is still cool. Andy Weir, author of *The Martian*, followed this model. He released the book chapter-by-chapter on his blog. After reader demand, he uploaded it to Amazon for $0.99. It exploded and became a bestseller, then a Hollywood film.

The lesson? Own your release schedule, own your income. Serialization was the 19th-century version of a paid newsletter.

And that model is still thriving today.

Act III: Digital Patronage: The Paid Newsletter Kingdoms

Welcome to the era of direct-to-reader.

We're living in a time when writers no longer have to chase advances, beg editors for assignments, or rely on ads to monetize their work. Instead, they can go straight to the readers who value their words most. Paid newsletters have emerged as one of the clearest paths for writers to turn audience attention into real income, even after the deterioration of traditional publications.

Paid newsletter platforms have made the paywall model simple and accessible. Writers use them to serialize essays, share research deep-dives, deliver exclusive interviews, or even publish books in-

3. The Morgan Library & Museum, "A Letter from Charles Dickens," *The Morgan Library & Museum*, accessed 2025, https://www.themorgan.org/collection/A-Letter-from-Charles-Dickens/44

4. "Charles Dickens and His Cunning Manager George Dolby Made Millions from a Performance Tour of the United States, 1867–1868," *Docslib.org*, accessed 2025, https://docslib.org/doc/2286444/charles-dickens-and-his-cunning-manager-george-dolby-made-millions-from-a-performance-tour-of-the-united-states-1867-1868

progress. Readers pay for the content, but they also pay for access, voice, and the sense of supporting someone whose work they believe in. The platforms may come and go, but the concept and appetite from readers will remain the same.

Below are some of the writers who are finding success in their niche, but you can always scroll through the top newsletters on any given subject to see what's possible.

Stratechery: The Solo Analyst's Media Empire

Ben Thompson didn't want to work for a newspaper or an ad-supported blog. Instead, he built Stratechery, a one-man subscription newsletter offering in-depth business and tech analysis.

For around $10 a month, readers get thoughtful, well-argued essays breaking down everything from Apple's strategy to media mergers, often with frameworks now taught in MBA programs.

He has more than 40,000 paying subscribers, translating to over $5 million per year in revenue. No ads. No bosses. Just him, a paid newsletter, and an audience that values his brain enough to fund an entire media company of one.

Letters From an American: History as a Bestseller

Heather Cox Richardson was a history professor who began writing Letters from an American in 2019 to help readers understand the news through a historical lens. Her style is calm, measured, and deeply researched, which is a stark contrast to cable news shouting matches.

What began as a way to inform friends and family grew into one of Substack's most successful paid newsletters. At around $5 a month, her subscriber base likely earns her over seven figures *per month*, turning kitchen-table writing sessions into a media property read by millions, shaping conversations about American democracy in real time.[5]

The Quiet Middle Class of Newsletters

Beyond these headline-grabbing success stories, thousands of smaller newsletters quietly clear mid-six-figures annually. These six-figure newsletters fund full-time writing careers without the need for permission from editors, marketers, or advertisers. They let writers build sustainable businesses around their expertise, passion, and consistency, whether that's parenting advice, investigative journalism, or serialized fiction.

This section is just an introduction to the promise of this model, but not its step-by-step guide, which I'll cover later in this book. In Part Two we'll go deeper into the tactics, tools, and strategies for building a paid newsletter that supports your writing life.

The big lesson from the Creator Economy? The new Medici is the crowd. A thousand true fans with credit cards beat one flaky studio exec every time.

Why These Stories Matter Now

If you think you're at a disadvantage because you don't have a royal patron, think again. History is littered with examples of artists who got paid—really paid—by mastering both their craft and the distribution systems of their time.

But here's the thing: we're actually better positioned than any of them. This isn't just a pep talk. It's an argument for why the so-called "Creator Economy" is the best patronage system in history, if you know how to use it.

Here's why you've got a once-in-history advantage as a creative:

5. Katelyn Eckstein, "How Heather Cox Richardson Built a Paid Newsletter with Over 1 Million Subscribers," *Growth in Reverse*, accessed 2025, https://growthinreverse.com/heather-cox-richardson/

1. **History Proves the Model.** Creativity + distribution = revenue. The model is old as dirt, but your distribution channels are nice and shiny. Use it to accelerate your writing.
2. **Tools Are Dirt Cheap.** Your phone does what Gutenberg's entire factory couldn't. You've got every responsibility to hit "publish" on your work.
3. **Influence Is the New Infrastructure.** Traditional ad spend is declining. Brands want authentic voices, not agency bureaucracy and corporate copy-and-paste. Creators get the contracts.
4. **AI Automates the Boring Bits.** When robots write grocery lists, human storytelling becomes premium.

Artists have always made money by adapting to the channels of their day. The difference now is the channels are cheaper, faster, and wide open. You don't need a Pope, a Medici, or a Manhattan-based publishing gatekeeper. You need to understand the tools at your disposal—and be bold enough to use them. This is the golden age of writers who know how to sell their work without apology.

How to Join the Paid-Creator Bloodline

There's a lineage here from frescoes to social feeds.

If you want in, here's your roadmap:

1. **Choose Your Patron Path.** One sponsor? Many fans? A hybrid? Every example in this chapter fits one of these.
2. **Build a Flagship Asset.** That could be a serialized novel, a signature newsletter, a paid course, or a memoir service.
3. **Publish on a Cadence.** Dickens had chapters. Paid newsletters have weekly drops. Momentum is magnetic.
4. **Collect Email, Not Likes.** Algorithms bow to inbox ownership. That's why paid newsletters are superior to social media platforms that control who sees your content.

5. **Charge with Self-Respect.** Michelangelo didn't discount his day rate. Neither should you.

You live in the golden age of paid creativity. Your medieval predecessors needed a duke. You only need Wi-Fi.

The playbook is proven across empires, printing presses, and newsletter scrolls. The only variable left is you.

So pick a canvas. Set your rate. And paint the ceiling.

Power Move: Audit Your Potential Patrons

Make a list of the last five people who paid you for your creative work. Were they sponsors? Clients? Fans? Which model felt easiest, most energizing, most profitable? Now imagine doubling down. What would it look like to build your cathedral around that?

Haven't gotten paid yet for your creative work? Don't worry. Instead, go back through this chapter and see which writing business model looks most interesting to you. Write it down. We'll dive into money engines for writers in Part Two, which is just pages away.

Amy's Field Notes: Stop Worshipping the Struggle

In my early twenties, starving for your art wasn't just normalized, it was chic. It was the badge of honor we all wore in the assistant trenches. Over breakroom leftovers and half-sent emails, we'd swap war stories like medals: Who got screamed at this morning? Who stayed late rewriting an email for their boss's boss? Who cried in the stairwell and then got back on phones like a champ?

Suffering was our shared currency. And I was rich.

But one day, the illusion cracked in the most mundane of places: on a lunch break.

She wasn't just any fellow assistant. She was *the* assistant. The belle of the agency. Stylish in an effortless European way, with a faint accent that made everything she said sound like a TED Talk. She had negotiated higher pay than the rest of us (legend status), and in her free time she was learning to play the piano and uploading videos of her singing like some kind of Disney princess.

So when she invited me to walk to lunch with her one afternoon, I said yes, thrilled to be getting face time with someone who seemed to be hacking the whole system.

We walked. We chatted about the usual chaos. And then, halfway to overpriced lunch, I cracked open.

"Is this really supposed to be this miserable?" I asked her, trying to sound casual. But the desperation bled through.

She didn't flinch. Didn't pause. Just shrugged and said, "If you don't like it here, you should quit."

I laughed, kind of. My whole body tensed. Because what she said so casually felt impossible to me.

Quit? I couldn't just quit. I had rent. I had health insurance through this job. I had a career path that required me to eat shit now so I could feast later. I had a plan. A pipeline. A carefully stacked house of cards that relied on me keeping my head down, paying my dues, and hoping someone would eventually pluck me out of the pile.

Of course *she* could quit if she wanted to. She was well-paid, talented, magnetic. She could move through the world with power because she had some. Or so I told myself.

I spent the rest of that walk constructing a hundred arguments for why she was wrong and I was right to stay miserable. I clung to my pain like it was proof of progress, even as our conversation moved on to other topics.

But deep down, I knew.

She had power. I had excuses. She believed in her own mobility. I believed in gatekeepers. She had accepted that life could be better if she made bold choices. I was still playing the waiting game, hoping someone would choose me.

And while it would take me a while to act on that moment, the seed was planted. Eventually, I left that job. I left that entire industry. And I built a writing career not around begging for scraps but around setting my own rates, owning my time, and choosing clients who valued my brain.

Now, when I talk to aspiring writers or burnt-out creatives who are still operating under the myth that suffering is the cost of entry, I see the same tension flash across their faces. The same defensive monologue I once rehearsed on that sidewalk in Los Angeles.

And I get it. I really do. Starving for your art feels noble. It feels like part of the work. But that's the trick. The struggle can feel so familiar, so righteous, that you start to confuse it with meaning.

If this part of the book has stirred something in you—if your shoulders tensed or your inner monologue started building rebuttals —pause and take a beat.

Ask yourself: Is this resistance? Or recognition?

Because when you feel your defenses go up, it often means a deeper truth is knocking.

You don't have to follow my exact path. But if there's one thing I hope you take from this chapter, it's this: You are allowed to want more. You are allowed to leave when something is breaking you. You are allowed to get paid, get praised, and get free—all at once.

We were never meant to worship the struggle.

We were meant to write, build, create, and thrive.

And Part Two? It shares with you the money engines that will help you thrive and build the writing life of your dreams.

7

BUILDING YOUR MAGNETIC WRITING BRAND

Here's the truth I wish every writer learned at the beginning of their journey: your personal brand is the most valuable currency you have.

It doesn't matter if you're an author, a ghostwriter, a freelancer, a blogger, or any other type of writing professional. Your brand is the trust engine that turns strangers into readers, readers into fans, and fans into clients.

It's what's allowed me to land five-figure social media brand deals as a bonus to the work I'm doing elsewhere. To build companies. To charge luxury fees for ghostwriting. To have readers buy my books and pay to read my newsletter.

Every time I've invested in my brand—getting new photos, redesigning my website, refining my messaging—I've seen results. More interviews. Bigger bylines. New clients. Higher sales.

But here's the thing most people miss: you can't grow your brand separate from your writing. It's all intertwined. Your personal brand is the umbrella over everything you do.

I've had freelancers ask me, "Amy, should I have a separate website for my author brand and my freelance brand?"

My answer is always the same: No. Put it all under one roof.

Because your freelance clients want to see your writing. Your readers are curious about your expertise. Even if they don't 100% overlap, they'll both strengthen your reputation.

This chapter is for all of you. Whether you're selling books, client services, newsletter subscriptions, or all of the above.

Great Writing Isn't Enough (If No One Finds It)

Coming up in the Hollywood system, I was told a lie: *The cream rises to the top.* That if your writing was good enough, it would somehow be discovered. Agents would call. Readers would flock. Checks would materialize.

That myth serves a purpose, just not for you.

It's a story gatekeepers whisper to keep the slush pile full and the power asymmetry intact. If your book flopped, it's because you lacked skill. If your screenplay never got optioned, maybe your talent just needed more time.

Here's what's really true: distribution matters just as much as the quality of the writing, because quality work can't become a bestseller if no one reads it. That's why Hollywood routinely spends more promoting a film than actually making it. That's why publishers care more about your platform than your prose.

Your writing doesn't get discovered because it's good. It gets discovered because it's packaged and marketed in a way that readers recognize, trust, and want. That's where personal branding comes in.

Think of it this way: A Birkin bag and a $20 purse from Amazon serve the exact same function. They hold your stuff. But a Birkin signals scarcity, status, and value. There are waitlists for that bag. Auctions. Whole black markets.

That's what branding does. It turns ordinary into aspirational.

Your writing might be the best-kept secret on the internet. But if it doesn't look like something worth paying for and if it doesn't feel premium, urgent, or unmistakably you, it'll sit unread, unshared, and underpriced.

Branding is how great work gets traction. It's how writing

becomes a movement. And it's how you stop waiting for gatekeepers and start building your own demand.

Brand = Shortcut to Trust

Your brand is your cheat sheet for readers, clients, and partners. It's a promise you make (and keep) about what working with you or reading you will deliver. Branding isn't just logos or fonts. It's about consistency and trust.

Think about it like this:

- **Visual cues:** the colors, fonts, and photos you use signal tone and professionalism.
- **Verbal cues:** your voice, catchphrases, point of view—these make you recognizable.
- **Reputation cues:** screenshots of wins, client testimonials, bestseller lists—these prove you can deliver.

Branding is about familiarity, and familiarity sells.

The Obituary Test: Branding With the End in Mind

This exercise is a reality check disguised as a branding tool, and it might just be the most clarifying thing you ever do for your career.

Here's how it works: If you had to write your obituary today, based only on what you've done so far, what would it say? Would it celebrate the writer you *wanted* to be, or would it read like the résumé of someone who died still waiting to be chosen?

Now comes the uncomfortable yet liberating part of the Obituary Test. What's the gap between what your obituary would say today and what you want it to say someday? Do you want to be remembered for half-finished drafts and someday-I'll-start-that-book energy? Or do you want the headline to scream: *Author of bestsellers. Built a seven-figure writing business. Gave other writers proof to dream bigger.*

This isn't about morbidity. It's about clarity. Life is short, and your brand should reflect what matters most, not just to your bank account, but to your legacy.

Because here's the truth: if you want to be known for something, you have to tell people what that something is.

Here are some reminders when it comes to your brand:

- Your readers won't magically intuit that you're writing the next great memoir if your website still says "under construction" with no details about you and your projects.
- Your dream clients won't know they can pay you six figures to ghostwrite their book if your social media bio screams "will work for coffee."
- The world can't celebrate the writer you want to be unless you start signaling it loudly, consistently, and strategically.

This is the branding gap in action: where you are versus what you want to be remembered for. Your job is to bridge it with intention.

The Obituary Test strips away the noise. Suddenly, the fears that keep you from hitting publish don't matter. Neither does the comparison game on social media or the pressure to hop on every algorithm trend. What matters is this: are you moving closer to the legacy you want?

So grab a notebook and answer these questions:

- What do I want to be known for?
- What stories, books, or ideas feel non-negotiable for my life's work?
- If I died tomorrow, what would I regret not creating?

Write it all down. Then compare it to what your personal brand is signaling right now. If there's a gap, and there likely will be, that's your roadmap. That's the difference between being a writer who hustles for scraps and one whose name becomes shorthand for value, trust, and impact.

Branding isn't about fonts and filters. It's about aligning your current reality with the future headline you want the world to read when you're gone. And the time to start writing that headline? Today.

Let's look at some examples of branding in the wild of how strong authors leveraged their personal brands to turn their writing into empires to help you get inspired.

Ana Huang and the Rise of Lo-Fi Fandom

Ana Huang didn't need a glossy book tour or six-figure marketing plan. She built her romance empire the scrappy way, by posting her stories on Wattpad, self-publishing, and showing up consistently on TikTok. Her *Twisted* series caught fire with BookTok readers, racking up over 1 billion views and helping her sell 1.47 million print books in 2024 alone.[1] No ad budget required, just content that felt real, fan-first, and relentlessly consistent.

Here's the lesson: You need proximity, consistency, and a story worth telling. Show up where your readers are, and do it with care.

Brené Brown as a Vulnerability Expert

Brené Brown built a brand around one clear theme: courage through vulnerability. She's written multiple #1 New York Times bestsellers, hosts a top-ranked podcast, and commands speaking fees that start at $100,000.[2]

Lesson: A tightly defined message expressed consistently across books, podcasts, and keynotes compounds trust and demand.

Together, these examples prove that when readers know your name and your promise, they'll buy, binge, or book you—no gatekeeper required.

---

1. Jeff Nelson, "Author Ana Huang Is Twisting Up the Romance Genre — and Topping Best-Seller Lists Doing It," *People*, accessed 2025, https://people.com/ana-huang-books-twisted-king-of-sloth-8630875

2. Jamie Ducharme, "Brené Brown on How to Be a Better Leader," *Time*, accessed 2025, https://time.com/5441422/expert-feelings-brene-brown-leadership/

Don't let me show you what's considered to be good branding, though. There are many more authors making creative choices with how they attract readers, and I recommend following authors across their different channels to see what's working for writers now.

Face-Forward Branding vs. Pen Names and Mystery

Author brands can have a layer of complication when writers choose to use pen names, and I get a lot of questions about pen names from clients and fellow writers.

Here's my take: pen names can be useful. They give you genre flexibility. They can let you separate sensitive or adult work from other writing. They offer a layer of privacy if you need it.

Look at Lemony Snicket, a pen name that created intrigue and a strong brand around the book series *A Series of Unfortunate Events*, one of my favorite reads as a kid. But even Daniel Handler (the man behind Snicket) eventually parlayed that success back to his real name.

Because readers want *real*. The internet rewards transparency. It rewards you putting your name, face, and reputation on the line.

If you want faster trust, better writing jobs, and an audience who feels connected to you, I recommend writing under your real name.

You can always use initials if you want partial separation. But remember, if your writing takes off, you'll probably want to claim that success openly anyway.

So if you're comfortable, go face-forward. It's the best way to build a loyal, long-term audience.

Keeping Your Brand Alive: Staying Consistent

Here's the unsexy truth about branding: the magic isn't in the launch. It's in the maintenance. Consistency is the engine that makes your brand compound over time.

I know because I've lived it. For two years straight, I published my paid newsletter every single week through jet lag, deadlines, and days when my brain felt like cold oatmeal. And for most of that time, growth was slow. But then came the hockey stick moment: I figured out what my audience wanted, doubled down, and now that newsletter brings in six figures in annual recurring revenue. People stay subscribed for months because they trust the value. That trust was built drip by drip, week by week.

Same thing with freelancing. My early years were a slog of pitching and posting until momentum hit. If I could go back, I'd double down on committing to consistency sooner. Because when I finally did, my business exploded. That's the point of this book. I'm here to hand you the hard-won lessons I've learned so you don't have to spend years figuring this out like I did.

If you want outsized results, you need outsized consistency. And yes, it's hard at first. It feels like shouting into the void. But habits compound. The first few months take grit. Then it becomes your default.

Consistency builds familiarity. Familiarity builds trust. Trust drives sales.

Your brand is only as strong as your commitment to showing up. That doesn't mean burning yourself out or becoming a content robot. It means picking the channels that matter most to your goals, and making your presence there inevitable.

Because here's the truth: the writer who shows up regularly, even with "pretty good" work, will beat the genius who posts twice a year and then disappears to brood in a café.

Consistency is the great equalizer. Nail it, and the world won't just notice you—it'll start looking for you.

Quarterly Audit: The Glow-Up Check

Every 90 days, look at your brand like you've never seen it before:

- Do your bios still reflect what you do now?
- Is your headshot current—or does it scream "2016 LinkedIn energy"?

- Are your offers and rates up to date?

This is also the time to ask: Do I need a site refresh? New photos? Better positioning? Brands don't just age, they expire if you don't give them oxygen.

Optional But Powerful: SEO/GEO and Blogging

Newsletters are great, but they live in walled gardens. Blogs get indexed better than paid newsletters (even if your newsletter has a website component), which means your future clients and readers can stumble on you via Google (thanks to search engine optimization, or SEO) and AI-powered search (which some people refer to as generative engine optimization, or GEO). SEO and GEO are both still part of my arsenal of secret weapons that I've relied on for years to get traffic into my writing business.

If you can manage it, post at least once a month or batch content for your blog quarterly that hits the keywords your ideal clients and readers are searching for on search engines or AI-powered tools. But don't stress if this feels like too much. Every niche is different, so focus on where your audience hangs out most.

4 Personal Branding Missteps to Avoid (And Why They're Sabotaging You)

First, let me say this: you're going to be imperfect, and that's okay. Your brand is a living thing, not a marble statue. You're going to experiment. You're going to pivot. Sometimes you'll post something that makes you cringe three weeks later. That's called growth.

So don't beat yourself up. But there are a few predictable mistakes I see writers make again and again, and they're worth sidestepping if you want better results, faster.

1. Inconsistent Voice

One day you sound like a Yale literature professor. The next, like a brain rot teen with a caffeine addiction. The problem? Readers don't know which version of you they're getting, or if they can trust either one.

However, you can adjust tone slightly for different audiences. Your ghostwriting clients may want buttoned-up clarity. Your romantasy readers want swoon and sass. But if your voice is whiplash-inducing across platforms, you confuse people. And confused people don't buy.

The real culprit? Most writers who struggle with consistency don't actually know who they are as a writer yet. It's just part of the work you need to do. Figure out your voice, then anchor everything to it.

2. Visual Whiplash

Your social media grid looks like a ransom note. Your newsletter screams "corporate minimalist" one week and "unicorn rainbow fever dream" the next. Random fonts. Clashing colors. Graphics that look like they were designed during a power outage.

Visual inconsistency signals chaos, even if your writing is brilliant. You don't need a Madison Avenue agency to design your graphics, but you do need a cohesive look. A few consistent brand colors. A font family you love. And yes, hiring a designer early can pay off fast. (Real talk: part of why my Substack sprinted ahead of others? Branding. Mine had personality and looked like a human made it with some love and intentionality.)

3. Disappearing Acts

You were posting weekly. Then life happened. Six months later, you resurface with a "Sorry I've been MIA!" post nobody was waiting for.

Listen: breaks are fine, as mental health matters more than algorithms. But vanishing for months at a time kills momentum. People forget you exist. Or worse, they assume you quit. Even if you need to go heads-down on a project, keep some kind of heartbeat: a quick newsletter, a placeholder post, something that says, I'm still here, still building.

And yes, I practice what I preach, even when it sucks. The sickest I've ever been in my life was in Athens, Greece. Picture this: I'm running a high fever, wrecked with autoimmune flare-ups, delirious in bed watching *Bachelor in Paradise* with Kyle and wondering if this is where my story ends. I felt like death's understudy.

And you know what? I still wrote and published my weekly newsletter that week. Not because I'm a masochist. Because I'd made a promise—to my audience and to myself—that I would show up every single week. I haven't missed a week in almost three years, and it's a core element of my success. But the point I'm trying to really hammer home here? That payoff started with one simple rule: *consistency beats perfection.*

Even when it's not your best work. Even when you'd rather watch reality TV and spiral. Hit publish anyway. People want your real self to show up. Authenticity plus consistency is a trust compounder, and trust is what sells books and lands premium clients.

And if you want to learn from my mistakes, here's one: build better systems than I had. Don't wait until you're feverish and horizontal to realize you need a backup plan. While I've stayed consistent no matter what, I've since learned there's a smarter, saner way. You don't have to be a martyr for your momentum. As James Clear puts it, "You do not rise to the level of your goals. You fall to the level of your systems."

Consistency is powerful, but it's the systems underneath that make it sustainable.

4. The Value Vacuum

If your feed is all selfies or a relentless stream of "buy my thing!" posts, you're leaving money (and goodwill) on the table. People don't follow you to be an unpaid hype squad. They follow you for a reason: insight, inspiration, education, or entertainment. If your content doesn't hit at least one of those, you're basically background noise.

Power Move: Craft Your Brand in 15 Minutes

Now that you've read what *not* to do, let's focus on what you should do when crafting how you show up online. And no, you don't need a three-day retreat or fancy consultant to figure out your brand. Give me 15 minutes and a notebook, and I'll give you the first steps for building a powerful presence. Ready? Let's go.

Step 1 (5 Minutes): Define Your Promise

What's the one thing readers, clients, or students can always count on you for? Clarity beats cleverness here.

Examples:

- "I help founders tell their stories through books that get them speaking jobs and media features."
- "I write thrillers that make you lose sleep—in the best way."

Write one sentence. Make it specific. That's your North Star.

Step 2 (5 Minutes): Know Your People

Who are you talking to?

Jot down:

- **Who they are.** Are they time-strapped executives? Romance readers looking for escape? Freelancers chasing freedom?
- **Where they hang out.** What social media channels? What groups? What in-person events?

- **What they want.** What problems are they trying to solve
  —or what fantasies are they desperate to escape into?

When you know what keeps your people up at night (or what makes them click "buy" at midnight), your brand stops being noise and starts being a magnet.

Step 3 (5 Minutes): Draw Your Line in the Sand

Every strong brand stands for something, and just as importantly, against something. This creates tension, clarity, and memorability.

Ask yourself:

- What does my brand fight for? (Creative freedom? Diverse voices? Stories that spark hope?)
- What's the villain in my brand story? (Gatekeepers? Corporate drudgery? Generic content mills?)

Example:

- I stand for helping writers build wealth and power.
- I stand against the starving-artist myth and the gatekeepers who profit from it.

Write down your for/against statement. This becomes the emotional core of your brand message.

That's it. 15 minutes, three sprints, and you've got:

- Your promise.
- Your audience.
- Your stance.

This is the skeleton of your personal brand. Flesh it out as you go, but start here. Action beats perfection, and clarity beats overthinking every time.

Amy's Field Notes: Your Aura as an Asset

A few months ago, I was teaching a virtual workshop for a digital nomad group. I titled it something like "How to Make Writing Your Job." It wasn't a conscious branding move. It's just what I say. It's how I think. It's the phrase that's shown up in every part of my work for years now, from my Substack title to the dinner parties where someone asks what I do and I answer, "I help people make writing their job."

After the session, a writer posted on social media, saying something to the effect of, "I didn't even know you were the one teaching, but when I saw the title, I thought, this sounds like Amy. And then I showed up, and it was you. Of course it was."

That's branding. Not because my face was on the slide deck or because I had some clever tagline. But because my ideas were familiar. The language, the mission, the ethos all pointed back to me before my name ever did.

The truth is, I've always been "the girl who made writing her job." Even when I was broke and experimenting. Even when I was ghostwriting memoirs during the week and teaching yoga in South Central LA on weekends. Even when I didn't have the phrase fully crystallized, I was living it. Writing was always the engine behind the life I wanted. And my personal brand, if you want to call it that, has always been me trying to reverse engineer that engine and hand people the keys.

And yeah, I've been told more times than I can count that I was "doing too much." That I needed to pick a lane. That trying to be a novelist and a ghostwriter and a newsletter author and a founder was diluting my brand. But I don't buy that. Because when you zoom out far enough, the lane is obvious. It's storytelling. It's transformation. It's teaching people how to use words to build wealth, power, and freedom—whatever that means in their world.

I've never been one thing. I was a competitive ballroom dancer. A pole dancer. A part-time yoga teacher. An obsessive builder. A romantic at heart writing fantasy novels and detective short stories.

And instead of hiding the complexity, I've let it inform how I show up. Because the people who hire me, who read me, who follow me aren't looking for sterile, single-focus operators. They're looking for dimensionality. For someone who's lived a few lives. For someone who's built a body of work, not just a résumé.

One of my memoir clients told me she hired me because I'd written both fiction and nonfiction. That variety gave her confidence I could handle the nuance of her story. That was a turning point for me in realizing that brand could be something more than a narrow descriptor.

But your brand also changes.

I remember sitting in a comedy show in San Francisco in 2021 where a group of techies were using an AI prompt generator to roast audience members in real time. At one point, someone fed the tool a fake startup idea and it spat out a landing page headline. And I thought, wow, that's actually not bad. I'd spent years writing copy just like it. And in that moment, I knew I was done with copywriting as my main niche. Not because I was scared of AI, but because I saw where the wind was blowing. And I wanted to spend my energy in a niche that was more future-proof.

So I pivoted. I doubled down on the parts of my brand that couldn't be automated. Ghostwriting memoirs and long-form content. Building community. Teaching live. Writing essays that sounded like they were pulled straight from my bloodstream. Things that only I could do in only the way I do them. (And if you're worried about AI, don't be. Even if you *are* a copywriter, there are lots of opportunities out there for you. More on this topic in Part Three of this book.)

For the best writers, a living brand evolves. It listens. It responds. And it keeps the same spine even as the chapters change.

These days, I'm less interested in defining my brand in a single sentence. It's not a pitch. It's an *aura*. People might know me as the Substack girl. The memoir expert. The one who tells writers they can build seven-figure careers without gatekeepers. The woman who shows up, even with a fever, to send out her Sunday newsletter from a hotel bed in Greece. They know the rhythm of my work. The tone of my voice. The undercurrent of urgency in everything I write.

That's what sticks.

So if you're trying to figure out your brand, maybe stop looking for a perfect definition. Start asking: What am I known for? What do people say when they refer someone to me? What themes keep surfacing across everything I write, say, teach, or build?

Your brand is the experience people have when they bump into your work out in the wild and think: this feels like you.

You don't have to be for everyone. You just have to be unmistakable.

And that kind of clarity? That kind of consistency? It's not just good marketing. It's a magnet.

PART II

HOW TO BUILD THE MONEY ENGINE

8

BECOMING A "CREATOR CEO"

W hen I graduated from USC and landed in Hollywood, the first thing every agent, manager, and industry gate-keeper told me was: *"Don't worry about the business stuff. Let us handle it. You just write."*

Sounds dreamy, right? That's the siren song of traditional systems. You write, we'll do the rest. You stay in your creative bubble, and they'll handle the hard, boring stuff like contracts, checks, and marketing.

I believed that myth for years.

Because honestly? The thought of hiding in my own world of characters and ideas, letting someone else pitch my work and fight my battles sounded incredible. That's why so many writers flock to traditional publishing or studio systems. They think it means they can avoid the messy, business-minded part of this career.

But here's the truth: that world is gone.

Even in traditional publishing, authors are hiring their own publicists and social media marketers—often going into debt for a shot at a bestseller list. I recently saw a writer post about maxing out her credit cards just to pay for a PR team because her publisher offered zero marketing support.

Hollywood is no different. When I signed with my first managers, I thought they'd flood my inbox with meeting invites. Instead? Most of my own breaks came from social media reach-outs I did myself. From building relationships online. From showing up, creating, and sharing.

The system that promised to "take care of everything" doesn't exist anymore—and honestly, maybe that's a good thing. Because when you give up control, you give up power. You give up the ability to shape how the world sees your work.

That's why this chapter exists. To show you what happens when you stop waiting to be chosen and start running your career like a business—without losing your soul in the process.

You're not a passive writer.

You're stepping into your power as a **Creator CEO.**

What Even Is a Creator CEO?

A Creator CEO isn't just a cute term. It's a mindset shift. A strategy. A survival tactic.

If you run a paid newsletter? You're already halfway there.

If you self-publish, pitch clients, or monetize your writing in any way? You're already doing CEO moves.

But here's the catch: creating isn't enough. Being an artist alone won't guarantee income, sustainability, or freedom. The Creator CEO builds an engine around their creativity. They own their monetization, their distribution, and their destiny.

You don't need an MBA. You need clarity, boundaries, and the courage to run your art like the valuable business it is.

Creator CEO vs. Starving Artist

Let's make it plain:

- The Starving Artist waits to be chosen. The Creator CEO chooses themselves.

- The Starving Artist fears "selling out." The Creator CEO knows selling = sustainability.
- The Starving Artist hides behind the craft. The Creator CEO honors the craft and markets it boldly.

This is about creating a life where you can sprint hard when needed, and take a week to reset by the beach whenever you want. Freedom isn't an accident. It's a system.

Effort ≠ Wealth: Leverage Does the Heavy Lifting

If hard work alone wrote paychecks, the richest people in the world would be janitors, nurses, and EMTs.

But that's not how it works.

High earners rely on leverage. In tech, it's code. In finance, it's capital. For writers, it's our IP.

One manuscript isn't just a single thing you sell once. It's the master key to dozens of doors. If you stop treating it like a lone oak and start treating it like a timber company, you can harvest it over and over again—without planting a single extra seed.

That's leverage.

And this chapter will show you how to work smarter, not just harder. How to see your book as the starting point for a plethora of products, experiences, and revenue streams.

The Love and the Leverage: Balancing Artist Mode and CEO Mode

A master watchmaker once handed his grandson two nearly identical watches and asked, "Which one do you like better?"

The boy studied them, turned them over in his hands, and finally pointed at one.

"This one," he said.

"Why?" asked the watchmaker. "They're the same."

The boy shrugged. "I don't know. I just... like it better."

The watchmaker smiled, opened the back of the chosen watch, and revealed a secret engraving with a small heart: *for my love.*

Even without knowing why, the boy picked the one infused with care.

That's what readers feel, too. Authentic craft leaves fingerprints. It lingers in the lines, hums under the surface. And that means something important: if you want to build a writing career that lasts—and a brand that resonates—you can't lose the love.

But here's the other truth: love alone won't sell your book, build your audience, or fund your next creative sprint. Passion without systems equals burnout.

Enter the dance between Artist Mode and CEO Mode.

Why You Need Both Modes (And Why Most Writers Fail at This)

Artist Mode is when you create. When you fall down the rabbit hole of research, scribble in cafés, chase sentences that light you up. Artist Mode demands presence. It hates distraction. You can't write your most original work if your mind is spinning with launch dates and royalty splits.

CEO Mode is when you zoom out. When you look at your book not just as art but as an asset—a first step for offers, spin-offs, revenue streams, and rights deals.

CEO Mode asks hard questions:

- How will this book find its readers?
- How do I package it?
- What do I own—and what will I license?

If these two roles go to war in your head, you'll either:

(a) write brilliant manuscripts that never sell, or

(b) crank out soulless content because you're too focused on metrics to remember why you loved writing in the first place.

The solution isn't blending them—it's giving each role its season.

Protect your creative bubble when you're drafting. Guard it like a dragon on a pile of gold. Then, when the work is locked, switch hats and run your writing like a business. That's how you scale without losing your soul.

Designing a Writing Business You Actually Love

Here's where most "business advice for creatives" falls flat: it assumes you want to build a corporate machine. You don't. You want a life you're obsessed with.

James Patterson is an extreme example. He's morphed into a one-man publishing conglomerate who outlines obsessively, hands 50+ page treatments to ghostwriters, and ships more titles in a year than most authors manage in a lifetime. Some writers find his system genius. Others find it soulless.

Good news: you don't have to run your empire like James Patterson if that's not how you want to run your ship. You can keep your fingerprint on every word, if that's what lights you up. Or you can delegate the parts you hate—marketing, admin, cover design—to free up more time for what matters most.

That's the point of being a Creator CEO: you design the game.

- Hate drafting? Build a co-writing team.
- Love being hands-on? Keep it lean and hire help only for the tech headaches and things like bookkeeping.
- Dream of summers in Greece writing your next novel? Structure your offers and recurring revenue so you can disappear to the Mediterranean for a month eating grapes on boats without watching your business burn.

The question isn't "What's the right model?" The question is: what model gives me the most joy—and the most freedom?

How to Switch Between Creator and CEO Without Losing Your Mind

Think of it like a toggle switch:

- Drafting a first novel? Full Artist Mode. Shut out the noise. Ignore the algorithm.
- Post-launch planning? CEO Mode all the way—budgets, funnels, partnerships, press.

Some days you'll have to pivot between the two and brainstorm a new chapter in the morning and approve a cover mockup in the afternoon. But as you grow, aim for separation. Block whole weeks or months for creation, then whole weeks for execution. That's the dream: the flexibility to go all-in on art, then all-in on strategy.

One day, that might look like having a picnic in the park with your family as you clock out early, knowing your newsletter, ads, and client projects are humming without you. These systems buy you space to make better art.

One Book, Infinite Doors

Here's the mindset shift most writers miss: a book is not the finish line. It's the launchpad.

Whether you're writing a steamy romantasy trilogy or a nonfiction manifesto on leadership, that single manuscript is a master key. It unlocks dozens of doors—revenue streams, opportunities, and creative projects you never imagined when you typed "Chapter One."

This is the philosophy of a Creator CEO: you plant one seed, then you harvest for years.

Let's make this real. If you write fiction, you're creating a world and a playground for superfans. That world can spill out into limited-edition hardcovers, exclusive character art, themed jewelry, or collector's boxes. I've seen romantasy authors throw masquerade balls that feel like stepping into their books: immersive experiences with costumes, vendors, merchandise, and live actors. Fans will fly across the country for that kind of magic. And yes, you can create card games or puzzles set in your universe.

If you write nonfiction, your book is a calling card. It's a credibility engine that fuels everything else. That book can turn into a speaking career, high-ticket consulting, online courses, corporate workshops, or even physical products that align with your message. Marie Kondo started with a book and spun it into a global lifestyle brand around tidying up, with TV shows, product lines, and certification programs for other organizers.

One book. Infinite doors.

The George Lucas Playbook: Rights Over Raises

In 1976, George Lucas made a move that rewrote Hollywood's playbook: he gave up a $500,000 pay raise in exchange for something the studio considered worthless: sequel rights and 100% of the merchandise revenue. Fox executives thought they'd won. Toys for movies had flopped before. They assumed Lucas just wanted bragging rights.

What Lucas wanted was ownership.

Those "worthless" rights minted over $100 million in toy sales by Christmas 1978. Today, Star Wars merchandise alone has generated more than $29 billion, and the total franchise value sits near $47 billion. When Lucas sold Lucasfilm to Disney for $4.05 billion in 2012, his success was built on his created leverage. That single clause in his contract bankrolled his company Industrial Light & Magic, films like *The Empire Strikes Back*, and his creative freedom for life.

Here's the lesson: equity beats salary. Always. Lucas traded half a million dollars in short-term cash for billions in long-tail upside. Intellectual property multiplies things like movies into toys, toys into rides, rides into streaming empires.

And now, you don't even need a studio to unlock that leverage. In the Creator Economy, you can publish your book, keep every right— print, audio, merch, foreign, film—and build your own IP flywheel. That's what empires are made of.

If you want to be more than a wage worker in a pretty font, keep your rights. Treat them like oxygen in a locked room, because without them, your creative empire suffocates before it ever breathes. The upside is massive, and every spin-off, license, or product built from your world should have your name on the checks.

Lean Into Your CEO Side

You don't need a big publisher or a Hollywood studio to make this real. You just need vision—and the willingness to lean into your CEO side to make it happen.

Maybe your version is simple: your book becomes a lead magnet for coaching clients. Or a membership community. Or a newsletter with a paid tier where superfans get behind-the-scenes access. Or maybe you dream bigger: live events, immersive retreats, licensing deals, merch collaborations.

And here's the kicker: the creative spark you need to dream up these spin-offs? That's still art. That's still your genius at work. The difference is you're giving that creativity more oxygen by building systems around it.

You don't need a ton of business knowledge to implement this. You just need to start asking one question after every project: *"What else can I create from this?"*

Because when you answer that question, your book becomes what it was always meant to be: not an endpoint, but an empire.

Power Move: The Sunday CEO Hour

Artists make magic. CEOs make systems. You need both.

Here's your new non-negotiable: block one hour every Sunday for your CEO hat. No drafting, no tinkering with sentences. This is empire time where you step back from the keyboard and look at your writing business like a Fortune 500 company in miniature.

Your CEO Hour Agenda:

- **Check the Numbers.** Check the health of your writing business. Examine revenue to date vs. target, expenses, and runway. If you want a seven-figure year, you need math, not just vibes.
- **Audit Your Assets.** What have you built this week that compounds? Books, newsletters, courses, evergreen content—assets print cash long after you hit publish.
- **Spin-Off Scan.** What's the next door your book can open? Speaking gigs, merch, VIP experiences, licensing. If Lucas turned lunchboxes into billions, you can turn chapters into revenue streams.
- **Marketing Pulse.** What's fueling your pipeline? List growth, social proof, content rhythm. Fans can't buy if they don't know you exist.

From there, leave space to journal on what might move the needle forward, and then close the book on your CEO time to re-enter your creative headspace.

Amy's Field Notes: Honor the Work, Then Be the CEO

When I was studying screenwriting at USC, I got paired with a faculty mentor I didn't know well. He wasn't even one of my professors. But he gave me some of the best advice of my entire writing career.

The first thing he told me was: take a sticky note and write "Honor the Work" on it. Stick it on your computer so you see it every single day.

I did.

That phrase stuck with me. Even now, I think about it constantly. Honor the work. Don't shortchange the draft. Don't rush the heart out of it. Make it something you're proud of.

But my mentor didn't stop there.

He said: once you've honored the work, you need to switch gears. You need to run your writing career like a CEO.

He told me to make decisions as if I was running a business. To think about rights, pricing, contracts, marketing.

Even though I only met with him a couple of times, that advice changed so much for me. I return to it constantly, especially now.

Because that's the balance we're all trying to master. Honor the work. Then put on the CEO hat and share it with the world.

That's what this whole book has been about. Teaching you to own your talent, your business, your power.

It's not either/or. It's both.

And you're the only one who can do both for your own career.

9

HOW TO BUILD A LUXURY GHOSTWRITING BUSINESS

W hat is ghostwriting, really?

It's part performance, part alchemy. You step into someone else's voice like it's a tailored suit, disappear into their syntax, and re-emerge with a manuscript or other type of written deliverable that they'll call their own.

Done right, ghostwriting is more than writing. It's strategic translation. You take lived experience and render it into narrative power. The founder becomes a thought leader. The memoir becomes a legacy piece. The product is theirs, the fingerprints are yours.

And here's the magic: anyone with storytelling chops can do this. Great freelance ghostwriters just need curiosity, empathy, and the ability to ask better questions than most therapists.

If you're new to selling your skills as a freelance writer and want the full primer on how to get started, check out my membership and writing job board at MakeWritingYourJob.com or my book *Six-Figure Freelance Writer*. But even if you're just starting out, this chapter will hand you the keys to one of the most lucrative, fulfilling writing careers on the planet.

Freelance ghostwriters get paid for two things: our ability to vanish, and our ability to embody. In this chapter, I'll be focusing on

different forms of freelance ghostwriting, since it's the most emotionally resonant—and often the highest-ticket—form of freelance
writing.

While I specialize in memoir ghostwriting, I'll also touch on adjacent niches like social media ghostwriting and content ghostwriting,
where you're not writing entire books but crafting narratives in bite-
sized form: text-based social posts, newsletters, thought-leadership
articles, and more. Before I went all-in on memoirs, I spent years in
the content and copywriting niches, so I know how to help you crush
it at any of these forms of freelance writing.

All of these niches are part of the same ecosystem, and the goal is
the same in ghostwriting: to capture someone's voice, elevate their
message, and help them show up with clarity and authority. To step
inside another person's perspective—their rhythms, their jargon,
their sense of humor—and then deliver a story that feels like home.

From Madeira Sunrises to Vienna Rooftops

The sun was just beginning to rise on the Portuguese island of
Madeira. A faint line of gold cut through the ink-black Atlantic
outside the window of the renovated hotel just steps from the beach I
had called home—a sleek, modern hub designed for digital nomads,
complete with a cozy coworking space.

Kyle and I had spent the past few weeks swimming in the ocean
every morning, working with sea views in the afternoon, and winding
down with sunset walks alongside the cliffs and waterfalls. It was late
summer, and Madeira felt like a dream. Tropical. Tranquil. Alive.

But this particular morning, my routine was interrupted in the
best way.

My driver pulled up just as the sky began to shift from lavender to
peach. He whisked away my luggage as I got into the black leather
interior of the shiny Suburban, and we slipped into the early dawn.

I was off to the airport because a client was flying me out for a
last-minute memoir project in Vienna. They paid for everything—
airfare, transportation, accommodations. This isn't unusual in my

line of work. When you write books that capture the full arc of a life, clients want you close enough to catch the details.

By midday, I landed in Austria. The air was warm and breezy with remnants of the late-summer heat. As we drove into the city, Vienna stunned me. Its buildings didn't just stand, they performed. The architecture felt like sculpture in motion. Everywhere I looked, the city pulsed with elegance and history. It was like stepping into a symphony made of stone and glass.

My cozy rented flat was in a vibrant, waterfront neighborhood buzzing with cafes, boutiques, and bakeries. The flat itself was a dream with angled skylights, polished wood floors, and a rooftop patio with a view that stretched across the skyline.

That night, I ordered a wood-fired margherita pizza from a local neighborhood spot and ate it on my terrace as the city glowed under the setting sun. My notes were spread out on the wrought iron table, a glass of gifted fresh juice from my host beside me. In a few days, I would meet my client in person for the first time—someone I had only ever seen through a Zoom screen—and I would begin a week of deep-dive interviews for their memoir.

This wasn't just a book project. It was a legacy artifact. My client, a founder, wanted to capture the real story behind the company they helped build—not the press release version, but the truth. The mistakes. The mindset shifts. The family sacrifices. Their kids would read this book someday. So would their investors, co-founders, and future generations.

Before the work began, I made time to explore Vienna. I booked a photoshoot to capture new portraits for my website, as I was writing a travel blog about Vienna as well. I found a brunch spot with brioche so good it was borderline criminal. I also taught a live webinar about memoir ghostwriting from the living room of the flat, windows open, the sounds of Vienna filtering in from outside. In between, I dipped into bookstores, explored hidden courtyards, and lost hours in design shops filled with hand-stitched leather journals and minimal ceramic lamps.

Later that week, I met up with my client. They welcomed me into their home. Their family shared stories over plates of crisp schnitzel and fluffy dumplings. They took me through their trendy neighborhood, showed me the park filled with people out for evening walks, and offered homemade desserts as we talked about my client's early career. I saw the world that shaped them. I heard the parts of their story that didn't make it into investor decks. And I realized, again, just how lucky I was, as this was my work and my life as a freelance memoir ghostwriter.

Ghostwriting has given me a front-row seat to some of the most extraordinary lives, and the freedom to design my own. No corporate badge. No middle manager. Just my LLC, my passport, and a wire transfer that would make a mortgage broker sweat. This is luxury ghostwriting. And it thrives far above the trenches where freelancers argue about ten-cents-per-word blog posts.

If you're interested in becoming a ghostwriter—of memoirs, social media content, newsletter content, video scripts, or other types of writing—then this chapter will break down how to do so—and how to get paid handsomely for your work.

Why Luxury Ghostwriting Beats Every Other Niche

If you're new to freelance writing, here's the lay of the land: freelance writing is the umbrella where you sell your services to clients who pay for them. Underneath the broader category of freelance writing are dozens of different formats that exist in different niches—specialized lanes you can pick based on your skills and interests.

There's copywriting (writing that helps businesses sell things), content writing (think blog posts and newsletters), scriptwriting (for podcasts, videos, documentaries), and more.

When done right, ghostwriting is one of the highest-leverage, highest-paid, and most creatively fulfilling niche on the menu, and here's why:

1. **Time Is the Ultimate Luxury.** High-net-worth clients will happily trade six or seven figures to buy back hundreds of

hours. Writing a memoir (or a business book) in particular is a massive lift, and they don't have the bandwidth—or often the skill—to do it well. You're not selling a book: you're selling their time back.

2. **Authority Is Priceless.** A sharp memoir, a polished keynote, or a killer social media presence positions your client as the voice in their space. You supply the words— they bank the clout, the podcast invites, the speaking fees, the perception of being ten steps ahead of the competition.

3. **Long-Term Projects Create Financial Stability.** Memoir and book ghostwriting projects often span 8-12 months, which means predictable cash flow and built-in runway. These aren't quick jobs, they're multi-phase collaborations. Even long-form newsletter posts and other types of content require time to nail your client's voice and messaging. Most ghostwriters work with 3-4 clients at a time (fewer if you're writing books), spreading out risk and revenue. And smart contracts include things like kill fees, so you're protected even if a client flakes halfway through, but be sure to talk to your lawyer on what you can do to be protected.

4. **The Infinite Content Flywheel.** One flagship book becomes dozens of spinoffs: newsletters, video scripts, podcast episodes, conference decks, ghostwritten op-eds. The same research powers a full content galaxy. When you ghost a book, you're often ghosting the entire brand voice that follows.

5. **AI Can't Replace a Soul.** Automated tools can spit out blog posts. But they can't interview someone's spouse, detect micro-tics in how they speak, or structure a narrative arc that makes readers cry. Luxury ghostwriting is human work. Taste, discernment, and empathy aren't programmable.

6. **You Build Deep Relationships with Power Players.**
Ghostwriting is one of the few writing niches that puts you inside the inner circle of founders, CEOs, VCs, and high-powered creatives. You get the raw version of their stories —including the stuff they'd never share with the world— and you earn their trust in the process. That trust leads to referrals, long-term partnerships, and sometimes even equity opportunities.

7. **You Learn from the Smartest People in the Room.**
When you ghostwrite for high performers, you're getting a front-row seat to how they think, lead, and solve problems. Every project is a private masterclass. Over time, their frameworks shape yours. You walk away wiser, sharper, and often rethinking your own strategy.

8. **You Work from Anywhere On Your Own Terms.**
Whether you're ghostwriting from a beachside coworking space in Portugal or a rooftop flat in Vienna, this niche offers full location independence. Clients don't care where you live, they care that the pages land polished and on time. That's freedom most freelancers don't realize is possible.

Luxury ghostwriting—especially memoir ghostwriting—is intimate, rare, and often once-in-a-lifetime for the client. You're helping someone process and preserve their entire life story. Most people only write one memoir. When they hire you, it's a big deal.

That said, other forms of long-form ghostwriting are incredibly valuable, too. Some clients need help crafting weekly newsletters that grow their audience and business. Others need video scripts that distill their frameworks into clickable, shareable content. Ghostwriting solves the problem of distribution which every founder and creator must figure out for themselves as they grow.

Luxury ghostwriting works because it meets clients at the intersection of status, strategy, and storytelling. You help them shape how the world sees them. In return? You get paid like a CEO.

Mindset Shift: From Freelancer to Private Wordsmith

Scroll social media and you'll drown in "clients are broke" posts. That's the wrong room.

Luxury ghostwriting lives in a completely different atmosphere, where founders drop $100,000 on a new website without blinking, and hire executive coaches, stylists, and ghostwriters in the same breath. In that world, writing is strategy. Story is positioning. And your role is to offer not just pages, but transformation.

To succeed here, you need to operate like a private wordsmith and a trusted creative partner who brings both literary talent and business fluency to the table.

To do that, here are three concepts you need to master that we'll discuss in this chapter:

1. **Stop pitching by the hour.** Hours are sand. Sell outcomes.
2. **Ditch one-off jobs.** Offer a concierge content package if that's what aligns with what you like to write. You can bundle deliverables like a combination of a memoir + newsletter + quarterly keynote deck.
3. **Lead with scarcity.** "I take on two clients per year." The right people lean in fast.

Luxury ghostwriting is about becoming indispensable. That requires knowing your audience inside and out (their goals, their pressure points, their industry), delivering exceptionally high-quality work on a clear timeline, and speaking the language of ROI. If they can see results—reputation, reach, revenue—they'll invest in you again and again.

As a ghostwriter, you're shaping influence. You're codifying legacy. You're becoming the secret weapon behind someone else's rise. Price and position yourself accordingly.

The 7-Step Quick-Start Blueprint for Your Freelance Ghostwriting Career

Let's break down the blueprint for your freelance ghostwriting career into these seven steps:

1. **Define the Signature Offer.** A memoir that doubles as a thought-leadership engine.
2. **Price for Transformation.** Price your services in direct proportion to your client's upside, not your effort.
3. **Source High End Clients.** Warm intros, private masterminds, investor dinners, or through targeted internet reach-outs.
4. **Turn a Discovery Call into a Done Deal.** Diagnose pain, prescribe your signature system, close with an initial deposit.
5. **Design a White-Glove Workflow.** Your signature method, weekly checkpoints, white-glove revisions.
6. **Upsells and Expansion Packs.** Ongoing newsletters, social ghosting, course scripts.
7. **Leverage Proof.** Case studies, anonymity agreements, redacted receipts, or anything else you can do to build trust without breaking NDAs.

The rest of this chapter hands you the full playbook, so let's dive into all of these seven concepts.

1. Define the Signature Offer

Before you can sell, you need an offer. Not a vague "I write stuff" shrug, but a clear, irresistible promise: here's what I'll deliver, here's the transformation, and here's why it's worth every zero on the invoice.

Think of your signature offer as the marquee on your creative empire. It's the single service that pays the bills, signals authority, and makes clients stop scrolling and start wiring deposits.

It's a container with:

- **The Deliverable.** What tangible thing does the client walk away with?
- **The Transformation.** How does it change their life, career, or bank account?
- **The Timeline.** How long until they get it?
- **The Price.** A number that makes your stomach flip (at first) because it reflects the real value, not just your typing speed.
- **The Promise.** Why this matters—the big payoff.

If you want to dive deeper into the art of the offer, Alex Hormozi's book *$100M Offers* is the textbook on the topic. But let me break it down without a single MBA buzzword.

Here's my signature offer as a memoir ghostwriter so you can see what I mean:

- **Deliverable:** A 60,000-80,000-word transformational memoir.
- **Timeline:** 8-12 months door-to-door.
- **What's included:** My proprietary memoir writing method, weekly chapter drops, two full revision rounds, back-cover copy, and introductions to top-tier PR and marketing partners for launch. I'm both a writer and book concierge to help my clients go from idea to ready-to-publish book.
- **Why clients love it:** Founders and high-performers are drowning in meetings and half-baked drafts. They hand me voice notes and chaos, and I return with a polished origin story they can parade on stages, in press interviews, and across their entire brand presence.

That's it. Simple, luxe, and loaded with ROI.

But what if you're not into memoir ghostwriting? Write what excites you, and what clients will actually pay for. Love social strategy? Your signature offer could be an *Executive Ghost Package* with three long-form thought-leadership posts per week, plus two signature essays per month. Obsessed with on-camera content? Try a *Launch Video Script Suite* with four binge-worthy scripts designed to turn a book or course into a full-blown media moment.

Same principle: the deliverable should move a needle clients already track—money, audience growth, media buzz.

I'll offer a quick pro tip and word of warning, however. More ≠ better when it comes to your offer. Don't Frankenstein five random deliverables together because you think "more options" equals more sales. It doesn't. Every extra deliverable is another hamster wheel. One high-leverage service beats a buffet of busywork.

When in doubt, start with one offer you can deliver flawlessly. Nail it. Scale it. Then stack on extras like newsletters, keynotes, or online courses once the first engine hums.

2. Price for Transformation

If you're still charging by the hour, let me stage an intervention. Hourly pricing is fine when you're hustling for your first $5,000 or even maybe $50,000 month, but this book is about seven-figure writing. You don't get there by tracking keystrokes like a caffeinated court stenographer. Luxury ghostwriting is priced *by the transformation.* Your client isn't just paying for your time. They're buying the ripple effect of the momentum you create for them.

That ripple effect could look like...

- The investor pitch deck that lands eight-figure funding, built from the credibility your book gives them.
- The business deals they'll close when their memoir becomes their calling card.
- The clarity they'll gain—and the legacy they'll leave—

because you distilled their chaos into a cathedral of sentences.

However, there's more here below the surface of just "charging a lot." A five-figure price tag isn't about padding your bank account. It demands a higher caliber of commitment on both sides of the transaction.

When your client invests at a high level to work with you, they show up. They dig deeper. They prioritize interviews with you instead of punting them for a golf tee time.

And you? When you charge more, you bring your A-game that makes your client's jaw drop. That number on the invoice reflects the standard you've set for yourself. A premium price forces you to truly be excellent. It demands you to step up your writing.

Pricing high will also preserve your mental health. Cheap rates attract chaos clients—the ones who ghost you mid-chapter and demand refunds because Mercury is in retrograde. Premium rates attract decision-makers who value your craft and respect your time.

Charging more makes both the client and you, the writer, show up and commit to making the project great. Because when it comes to pricing, setting your rates is a head game. If you're sweating through your shirt before you hit send on that proposal, welcome to the club. Every writer faces the *oh-God-am-I-worth-it* spiral.

That's why we did the mindset drills in Part One of this book. You need to step into an alter ego when you quote your price. You need to become the version of you who already owns the outcome, the testimonials, the case studies.

Confidence is a muscle. Flex it until it stops shaking.

And here's the test:

If your price quote doesn't scare you a little when you say it out loud, it's too low.

Aim for the highest number you can say with a straight face. Then practice saying it until the terror turns into thrill.

If you're just starting out, you can start your rates off on the lower side of things if you need to build confidence and a portfolio. No shame in that. But raise your rates with every project. Pricing is a staircase, not a flat sidewalk. With each client, you're stacking proof and swagger, so charge accordingly.

3. Source High End Clients

High end clients often aren't blasting "ISO ghostwriter" on public feeds. They operate behind warm introductions, referral loops, and discreet spaces where amateurs never get past the door. Sometimes they find you because your online presence radiates authority. Sometimes they slip through curated backchannels that only insiders know about.

One of those backchannels? The exclusive corner of the job board over at MakeWritingYourJob.com. We run what I call the "quiet club" of premium writing opportunities hidden behind a paywall so only serious clients and serious writers make it inside. Many of them come in with one goal: hire a high end ghostwriter from our community. These Featured Job listings often never hit the public web. They're not on big marketplaces. They're on our private board because our reputation attracts the caliber of client who values confidentiality and invests accordingly.

If you're not already inside, you're missing a lane where clients go looking specifically for writers like you. That's one magnet.

Of course, there are other ways to bring great clients knocking your door down. Authority attracts, so publish something that matters. Run a newsletter that drips insight like a slow IV. Share ideas that make decision-makers stop mid-scroll and think, *This person gets it.* Your writing should feel like a high end showroom, not a bargain bin. Highlight case studies. Share behind-the-scenes slices of your process. Tell the stories only an insider could tell. The goal? Make your presence so strong that by the time they contact you, the question isn't if they'll hire you, it's whether you have a spot available for them on your waitlist.

You can also go out into the world where high-end clients are. Premium clients cluster in places money goes to play. Not in comment sections, but in boardrooms, box seats, and back rooms of conferences that require name badges with metal lanyards. Think art fairs, founder summits, investor dinners, charity galas. You don't need their wardrobe or their yacht, you need proximity.

When you show up in those spaces, leave the hungry-vendor energy at home. Position yourself as a peer. Small talk about ideas, not invoices. The fastest way to repel a high end client is to smell like desperation marinated in hustle. Show up as someone who belongs, because you do.

If you're worried about gaining access to these spaces, know that you don't have to pay crazy private club fees to access great clients in person. One of the writers in our community met one of her clients at a grocery store. Another at a book event. Potential clients are everywhere, and when you believe that you'll start to see them.

Another way to bring clients into your orbit is through targeted word-of-mouth. Referrals are your silent sales team. Build alliances with the professionals who already orbit your dream clients, such as PR strategists, estate planners, brand consultants. Offer them value first: insight, introductions, solutions that make them look good to their clients.

If the pipeline feels dry, you need more faucets. That means one-to-many channels like articles, blogs, or essays that signal expertise to anyone searching. It also means one-to-one outreach, such as personalized notes to people who can greenlight your work or whisper your name in the right ear. Some channels are going to work better than others, depending on your format. In my experience, cold outreach worked better for landing content and copywriting clients, whereas my memoir clients all had to come into my orbit through a warm lead or from finding me on an Internet search. I've even had clients find me because AI search tools sent them my way.

No matter how you build your client roster, remember that you're playing a long game. Finding premium clients is about building a presence that magnetizes. You step into rooms where money and ideas collide. You multiply your reach through people who already hold the keys. Invest in things like your website and online presence to stop chasing clients. They'll start circling you like moths to a bespoke flame.

4. Turn a Discovery Call Into a Done Deal

A discovery call isn't just a "get to know you" chat. It's the moment you step out of the writer box and into the strategist chair. You're an architect walking a client through the blueprints of their dream house before they wire the down payment.

This call exists for one reason: to diagnose, not to dance around small talk. Upscale clients don't need a pen pal. They need a surgeon who knows exactly where to cut and how deep.

A discovery call is your chance to:

- Clarify what the client wants.
- Show you understand why they don't have it yet.
- Prove you have the exact map to get them there.

If you've magnetized properly (your content screams authority, your portfolio glows like a shiny boutique), this call should feel less like cold selling and more like a doctor confirming symptoms before writing the prescription.

Here is my **5-step framework for discovery calls:**

1. **Clarify the vision.** "What does success look like 12 months from now?" Get them talking about the endgame, whether that's a book launch, credibility boost, lead generation, or finally getting their story on paper without a nervous breakdown.
2. **Surface the pain.** "What's standing between you and that outcome?" Why haven't they done it yet? Time? Clarity? Tried before and burned cash on an amateur? Lock in those reasons. They'll become your anchor when objections show up later.

3. **Prescribe your process.** Walk them through how you help clients with surgical precision. Share details about things like macro and micro outlines, deep-dive interviews, chapter delivery cadence, revision rounds. Make it sound like a smooth private jet itinerary—everything accounted for, zero turbulence—and focus your process on outcome. Position yourself like a guide, helping your client get to where they need to go.

4. **Quote the investment.** State the number. Full stop. Just, "the investment for everything I shared with you is..." and then drop your quote. No nervous laughter, no discounting, no explaining your landlord's rent hike. Let silence work for you. Confidence in delivery signals confidence in price.

5. **Make the "yes" easy.** Send one clean package with your proposal, contract, and invoice so the next step is as simple as a click. The easier you make it to sign, the faster the deal closes.

If a cost objection surfaces, and it sometimes will when your rates are high, circle back to what they told you earlier in the call: "You said your biggest fear was another year of missed opportunities. This is how we make sure that doesn't happen." Be confident in yourself and your skills when you're answering questions and handling clients questioning elements of your proposal. Some of my biggest clients had lots of questions on discovery calls, but others just said yes after five minutes and then asked where to sign.

You can also use social proof on your discovery calls to help clients with their buying decision. Sprinkle in lines like: "Most of my clients come to me after wasting time with writers who weren't specialists. They end up paying twice, once for the rookie, once for the rescue mission. My job is to make sure you never pay the amateur tax."

Remember that closing is a process, not a pressure cooker. You might seal the deal on the call, but often you will close the deal on a follow-up email. That's fine. The key is leaving them certain you're the only logical choice, and sending a post-call proposal that lays out next steps like a roadmap. Think like a surgeon again: once the diagnosis is clear and the solution feels inevitable, signing becomes the path of least resistance.

5. Design a White-Glove Workflow

Luxury clients are buying peace of mind. They want to know what happens, when it happens, and how effortless it will feel. The goal isn't to drown them in dashboards or bury them in subfolders. The goal is clarity without friction.

Think of it like a Michelin-star restaurant: the guest doesn't see the chaos in the kitchen. They just experience perfect timing, flawless plating, and a sommelier who seems psychic. Your workflow should feel the same.

However, simple beats fancy when it comes to your process. Some writers hear "workflow" and panic-buy software. Don't. A seamless experience is not about complexity, and most luxury clients don't want to "log in" to anything. They want to text you, send you a voice memo, and trust that the magic happens without them babysitting the process.

Here's the real art: making the experience of working with you feel streamlined while keeping the engine organized on your end.

That might mean:

- A shared folder for deliverables that updates like clockwork.
- A short branded PDF outlining key milestones.
- A single email thread for questions instead of five apps fighting for attention.

Your process should answer those questions before they ask them. Certainty equals trust. And trust equals zero microman-agement.

When it comes to communication style, match theirs while protecting yours. High end clients vary wildly. Some will only email. Others live on text. Some love long calls. Others want zero calls after kickoff. Figure out what works for both of you, and then set boundaries early so the project stays on track. That doesn't mean just bending to clients, but also establishing how you will work and communicate with them.

In my own memoir workflow, I tell clients I work asynchronously once drafting starts. Every week they receive a new chapter in a collaborative doc. I include margin comments with questions and invite their feedback via voice memo or text instead of calls. Why? Calls drag me out of deep work. This system lets them respond on their schedule, keeps momentum flying, and still feels personal.

When your workflow feels frictionless, you become irreplaceable. A great system reinforces your value at every touchpoint. It says: this isn't a scramble. This is a masterpiece in motion.

6. Upsells and Expansion Packs

Here's the truth: you don't have to turn every client into a lifetime subscription. You can absolutely be the literary samurai and drop in, write a memoir or another type of written deliverable, bow dramatically, and vanish into the sunset. That's a valid business model. Some writers thrive on one-and-done projects because it keeps their calendar open and their creative energy fresh.

But if you love going deep with clients—or if the thought of helping their story ripple across more stages and platforms lights you up—you can offer add-ons that extend the transformation you've already started.

Think of it like building a house. The memoir is the foundation, but the client might need walls, a roof, and a deck where they can sip champagne while quoting their own book at cocktail parties. Those "extras" are where your upsells live.

Upsells work because once a client trusts you with their life story, you become the keeper of their voice. That's a rare commodity. They don't want to train a stranger to capture their cadence all over again. They want continuity, and that's what makes upsells effortless. And remember, these add-ons aren't about wringing clients for cash, they're about deepening the impact of what you've already created. A memoir isn't just a book—it's the nucleus of an entire thought-leadership empire. If you enjoy building out that constellation, this is your playground.

Still, let's be clear: this is a choose-your-own-adventure. If the thought of managing multiple deliverables feels like a migraine in a trench coat, stick to your signature offer. But if you like the idea of ongoing partnerships and predictable cash flow, here are some extensions to consider.

Your starting point for a potential upsell depends on your signature offer. If you're a memoir writer, newsletters and speeches are natural extensions. If you start with newsletters, the upsell might be ghostwriting a book based on the content of the newsletters. If you write video scripts, you can also pitch newsletter articles to go along with the videos.

The magic question is: what's the next logical step for the client once they have the first deliverable? That's your upsell.

Some writers turn these add-ons into an entire agency—memoirs, courses, social content, all under one roof. That's an option if managing a team excites you. If it doesn't, ignore this and keep your solo empire lean. There's zero shame in staying a "samurai" if you'd rather spend your time writing rather than herding freelancers. Plus, you can work out a referral network with other professionals who may give you a percentage of the projects you bring to them, creating another stream of income.

7. Leverage Proof Without Breaking NDAs

Your ideal client wants to know three things:

1. Have you done this before?
2. Can you be trusted?

3. Will this be worth the investment?

You need to answer all three, without torching client confidentiality. That's the tightrope of ghostwriting: the better your clients, the harder you have to work to prove you exist.

The first option? It's to find ways to make your credit visible. Some writers go the co-writer route: name on the cover, shared credit, slightly smaller fee. If that visibility matters to you, it's a valid play. Others ask clients if they can include discreet projects in their private portfolio.

Personally? I stay deep ghost for most projects. No name, no public nods, no leaks. My reputation comes from other lanes in my career, and that's one of the big reasons this book preaches a three-pronged system: luxury ghostwriting, self-publishing, and a paid newsletter.

When you grow all three, they feed each other like a growth loop:

- Your self-published book proves you can write (and sell).
- Your newsletter shows consistency, personality, and reach.
- Your ghostwriting income bankrolls both—and earns you high-level case studies (even if anonymized).

That trifecta builds a brand no NDA can erase.

Option two is having anonymized case studies. Highlight the outcome of the work, not the name. Example: "Helped a tech founder craft a memoir that launched to 20,000 presales and secured three keynote spots at major conferences."

Metrics matter. Audience growth, book sales, revenue impact—whatever signals ROI. You're selling outcomes, not adjectives. I've found that ROI is hard to measure, but if you're able to quantify the impact of your work, you'll always be booked and busy. Even if you can't show ROI for client projects, you can hit publish on your own work and prove impact in your own world. That's why tracking metrics for your own projects can pay off in more ways than one.

When you're a beginner, it can feel more challenging to get the wheels spinning. You can't fake social proof, but you can manufacture momentum. If you're starting from scratch, try offering discounted rates to your first few clients in exchange for the ability to feature their book and their results. You can also build authority through your own projects while you climb—publish a short book, start your newsletter, guest-write essays on platforms your audience reads.

You may be a ghost, but your reputation doesn't have to be.

Power Move: Architect Your Seven-Figure Signature Offer

Think of everything in this chapter—signature offer, pricing for transformation, discovery calls, workflows, proof, the whole shebang —and boil it down to one irresistible sentence. Why just one sentence? Because clarity closes deals, and if you can't articulate your value in a single line, clients will never remember (or repeat) what you do.

Here's your move: write a one-sentence pitch for your signature service.

Start with this fill-in-the-blank:

I help [type of client] turn [their chaos/problem] into [the outcome they want] through [your signature offer].

Example:

I help founders turn decades of hard-won lessons into memoirs that build legacy and authority.

This one-liner is your North Star. Put it on your site. Drop it in your proposals. Whisper it to yourself when imposter syndrome shows up with a megaphone. This is the spine of your seven-figure business.

This is how you stop being a freelancer and start being a force.

Amy's Field Notes: Your Ceiling Is Imaginary

I've been told by clients twice in my life that my rates were too low— once when I was a newer freelancer, and again when I was already charging six figures for books.

Here's the scene: I'm on Zoom with a client who wants his memoir ghostwritten—a full-on legacy artifact. We're talking in-person interviews, travel, hundreds of hours of research and writing, plus packaging his entire life story into a brand asset he can use for speaking gigs, investor decks, and family posterity.

I quoted him my rate at the time: $150,000. I delivered it with a sense of calm and confidence—and felt like I was pushing the upper limit of what was reasonable.

He nodded and said, "Yeah, that makes sense. But honestly? I think you're undercharging for this."

I tried not to let my jaw hit the desk.

After we ended the call, I just sat there for a minute, staring out my window. Processing. Because I thought I had hit the ceiling with that number. I thought it was already "too much." Turns out, the ceiling was imaginary.

What he understood—and what I had yet to internalize—was that luxury ghostwriting isn't a cost. It's an investment with compounding returns. That's hard to price. In many ways, it's price*less*.

A $150,000 quote might make sense for one project. Another might justify $700,000 or more. Every project is custom. Every client has different goals. The value they get can't be measured in your hours—it's measured in the doors it opens for them.

And here's the truth: the moment someone tells you that you're undercharging, it's your flashing neon sign to raise your rates. Aggressively.

I've had to keep relearning that at every stage. So don't let your own limiting beliefs set your price floor. Let the value you create do that for you.

That's the difference between a freelancer and a luxury ghostwriter. Between writing for a paycheck and writing for power.

Smash through your imaginary ceiling and keep going.

10

PAID NEWSLETTERS THAT PAY YOU

Think about a future where you write something you care about—your essays, your serialized fiction, your sharp takes on culture—and readers pay you for the privilege of reading it. Not once, not per click, but every month like clockwork. No gatekeepers, no algorithms throttling your reach. Just your words, your readers, and a steady stream of recurring revenue.

That's the promise of a paid newsletter, and it's a model rooted in publishing history. As you'll remember from earlier in the book, Charles Dickens and other authors built their empires on serialized subscriptions. What's changed is that now you don't need a printing press, a publisher, or a distribution deal. You're the writer, the publisher, and the brand. You decide what goes out, when, and how.

Here's why this matters: for the first time, writers have a direct line to readers, and the ability to turn that line into a business. A paid newsletter isn't just an email in someone's inbox. It's a membership. A community. A living archive of your ideas. It can be as simple as weekly essays or as expansive as a multimedia empire with audio, video, and subscriber-only chats. You set the format. You set the price. You own the relationship.

Fiction writers? You can serialize a novel like Dickens, but with far better lighting and Wi-Fi. Nonfiction writers? Teach, rant, report, or chronicle your journey behind the scenes. Want to launch a personal gossip column for your city? People are out there paying $10 a month for that exact thing. There are writers clearing seven figures doing this, turning their voice into a one-person media company.

The landscape is wide open. The tools are built for you. Platforms like Substack, Beehiiv, and others make it possible to publish and monetize with zero tech headaches. Your paid newsletter can cover your bills, fund your next book, or buy back your time. This format is a scalable pillar of a modern writing business, and the only limit is your belief and ability to take action.

In this chapter, we'll break down the fundamentals: how to structure your newsletter, what to offer, how to grow and convert readers, and why this is a cornerstone of the seven-figure writer roadmap. Use this as your direct path to independence, one paid subscriber at a time.

The Email That Made Me $1,000 Before Breakfast

As I'm writing this section, it's a Tuesday, and technically I'm "working." Which, on this day, meant two hours of laptop time before I wandered off with Kyle for an early afternoon adventure through Golden Gate Park. We strolled through the Botanical Gardens, had matcha in the outdoor café amidst the koi ponds and babbling brooks in the Japanese Tea Garden, and met up with my brother for dinner at a Korean barbecue place nearby.

For all intents and purposes, I'm taking the day off. And here's the kicker: that morning when I slipped on sneakers, I checked my email and saw another $1,000 drop into my business bank account from my paid newsletters. Not an invoice I had to chase. Not a client call I had to attend. Just predictable subscription revenue doing its thing every weekday while I brushed my teeth.

That's the power of a paid newsletter. When you do it right, it's like an ATM wired to your words.

As I shared with you earlier in this book, I started my first paid newsletter with a wild goal: hit $96,000 a year in recurring revenue, and I blew past $100,000 in annual recurring revenue during the writing of this book. Most of that is profit.

And now? The system practically runs itself. I hired a team at MakeWritingYourJob.com to keep the job board fresh and the community thriving. My role now? 2 to 4 hours per week, tops. I pop in to answer subscriber questions, brainstorm ways to level up, and host events like live classes and mastermind groups for our community. While I'm out exploring San Francisco or having brunch with friends, my subscription revenue is yet another income stream from my writing business that pays for my life.

Oh, and because I like having multiple flavors in my writing life, I also launched Sutoscience.com, a newsletter that's pure essays: my ideas, my musings, my unfiltered brain on the page. It's growing fast. I give it an hour a week to draft my Sunday post. Between the two, I spend less time maintaining my newsletters than most people spend doomscrolling on their lunch break, and these newsletters return more than social media procrastination ever will.

Here's the truth: neither of these happened overnight. MakeWritingYourJob.com took two years to shape into the membership model it is now—a private job board, a thriving writer community, and a lineup of subscriber-only perks. I made mistakes (you'll avoid them). I tested ideas (you'll take the best ones). And now, the engine hums quietly while I live my life.

This is why I added paid newsletters to the seven-figure roadmap in this book. They're more than "extra income." They're freedom machines and idea incubators. They let you fund your art without begging a single gatekeeper. They give you recurring revenue so you're not chained to one-off client projects. They buy back time for your voice, your books, your big ideas.

In this chapter, I'll give you the advice I wish I had on day one— the strategies that work, the traps to avoid, and how to turn a blank page into a subscription people happily pay for. Whether you want a membership-style community stomping ground, a personal essay space, or something entirely your own, this chapter is your shortcut.

Let's build the machine that writes your freedom checks.

How to Pick a Niche People Actually Pay For

Here's the truth: general newsletters for "everyone" are like gas station coffee: lukewarm, forgettable, and no one's coming back for a refill. The paid newsletter game runs on obsession, not obligation. If your readers feel like they could get the same thing anywhere else, they'll disappear before you finish your sign-off.

So, what's the fix? Pick a niche that makes people stick. And before you panic thinking this means you need to pigeonhole yourself into "Marketing Tips for B2B SaaS on Tuesdays," let me save you: sometimes your best niche isn't a topic, it's your taste.

That's the secret most writers miss. The hook might not be "recipes for busy parents" or "true crime analysis." It might be the way you mix ideas like cocktails: one part literary gossip, one part cultural critique, shaken with a splash of your unfiltered personality.

Some of the top paid newsletters aren't about the subject alone—they're about the voice driving the subject. People subscribe because they crave how that writer sees the world. That's good news for you: your taste, your lens, your quirks can be the brand.

SO, WHAT DOES THIS LOOK LIKE IN REAL LIFE?

Here are some of the ways writers might blend their experience with a topic they cover for their paid newsletter:

- A journalist covers Wall Street with the sharp tone of an investigative insider.
- A novelist serializes their next book, complete with commentary on what's working and what's failing in real-time.
- A cultural critic blends book reviews with dispatches from

their tiny house in the woods—and somehow makes both addictive.

- A "things I'm obsessed with this week" newsletter that curates novels, $12 candles, and philosophical hot takes like a chic mood board for the brain.

Your niche is a point of view, not a prison sentence. And yes, your newsletter will evolve. Your early niche is a launchpad: start specific enough that people know what they're paying for, then let it grow with you.

Build an Offer That Feels Like a No-Brainer

A subscription isn't a tip jar. It's a promise: pay me every month, and I'll give you something worth coming back for. If that "something" is fuzzy, no one's clicking subscribe. If it's overwhelming—stuffed with seventeen bonuses and a private members-only channel you never update—they'll cancel before you cash the first check.

Your job? Make the offer so obvious it sells itself.

Start With This Question: What Are They Really Paying For?

Spoiler: it's not volume. You're not trying to bury readers under PDFs and live calls like a Black Friday grab bag. People subscribe because they want clarity, transformation, or connection—not chaos disguised as "value."

Your paid newsletter can take two forms:

- **Broadcast Model.** You write, they read. Think essays, serialized fiction, industry breakdowns. Minimal moving parts.
- **Community Model.** You write plus offer interaction— comment threads, chats, maybe live Q&As.

I chose the Community Model with MakeWritingYourJob.com

because I wanted a thriving writer hub. But for my second newsletter, Sutoscience.com, I chose the opposite and leaned into the Broadcast Model: zero membership add-ons, just my ideas and the page.

Neither is better. It's about what fits your energy and your reader's expectations. Do you want to run a bustling club or a curated magazine? Pick one lane and own it.

Outline What They Get

Write it down in plain language:

- **Core content.** The main thing people are paying for. Essays? Reading lists? Behind-the-scenes dispatches from your book launch?
- **Community.** Private chat, comments, members-only threads.
- **Extras.** Workshops, Q&As, resource libraries. But only add what you can sustain without resenting your own newsletter.

Pro tip: Start lean. A newsletter that delivers one killer essay a week beats a newsletter that promises the moon and implodes by month two.

Give It a Spine: Your One-Liner Pitch

When you've stripped away the excess, write this sentence:

"This is a newsletter where I [share what] for [who cares about it] because [why it matters]."

Examples:

"This is a newsletter where I dissect the secret economies of creative work for freelancers who want to make more money without losing their soul."

"This is a newsletter where I send essays about books, art, and ambition for writers who want a little chaos in their inbox."

This sentence is your core value offer. It will guide what you say yes to, and what you ruthlessly ignore.

Don't Create a Monster You Hate

Here's where most writers go wrong: they pack their newsletter like a holiday buffet. Too much on the table, nobody leaves happy—including you. Resist the urge to "add value" by adding noise. A simple offer that delights beats an elaborate circus that burns you out.

Think of your newsletter like a restaurant menu. If it has two pages, people feel confident ordering. If it has forty laminated options and a suspicious sushi section? They'll bolt. Give your readers focus. Give yourself sanity.

The bottom line: clarity scales, complexity kills. Start small, deliver what you promised, and grow from there. Your offer doesn't need to be everything, just something irresistible.

Pick Your Platform Carefully

Think of your platform as the house where your newsletter lives. It's not just the front porch where readers knock. It's the plumbing, the wiring, and the locks on the doors. If the foundation is shaky, your whole subscription model wobbles.

When I say "platform" I'm talking about where your newsletter is hosted, how payments get processed, and who handles the boring-but-essential stuff like customer service. Translation: this is the system that makes sure when someone clicks "subscribe," the money lands in your account and the email lands in their inbox.

Different platforms offer different deals. Some will charge you a flat monthly fee, like rent. Others will take a percentage of your revenue, like a landlord who wants a cut of every dinner party you throw.

Higher fees can sting, but some platforms justify them by offering built-in discovery tools or recommendation systems that help you grow faster. Others give you total control but zero exposure, which means you'll be driving all your traffic solo. Neither is wrong. It's about which trade-off makes sense for your goals.

Before you commit, understand this: platforms change constantly. Fees shift. Features evolve. A platform that's hot today might be gone in two years. So do your research and check current terms before you sign up. And while you're weighing the pros and cons of ease, customization, and discoverability, remember this: you *must* own your email list.

If you take nothing else from this section, take that. If you can't download your subscriber emails at any time, you don't own your audience. And if you don't own your audience, you don't own your business—you're just squatting on someone else's land. A platform that locks up your list is one bad policy update away from vaporizing your revenue.

That's not a business model. That's an eviction notice waiting to happen.

This is why paid newsletters beat social media. An algorithm can decide whether your posts sink or swim, but emails? They go straight to the inbox of your readers. No gatekeepers. No roulette wheel. As long as you have your list, you can move platforms, pivot strategies, and still reach the readers who pay for your words.

So yes, obsess over design features and payment splits, but make subscriber ownership your non-negotiable. Everything else is just decor. Your platform is the delivery truck, but the email list? That's the engine. Never hand over the keys.

Price for Perceived Value, Not Your Effort

Pricing your paid newsletter isn't about counting keystrokes or timing your typing speed. Nobody cares if it took you ten minutes or ten hours to write an issue—they care what lands in their inbox and how it makes their life better, smarter, or more interesting. Readers pay for what they feel they're getting, not what you sweated behind the screen.

Think of it like this: your price tag signals the experience. A $15 latte feels different than a gas station drip, even if the caffeine molecules are the same. Your newsletter works the same way. You're not selling ink on a page—you're selling exclusivity, clarity, or entertainment they can't find anywhere else.

Different readers value different things. Some want the cheapest ticket to your brain. Others will happily pay extra to sit in the front row, snag VIP perks, and feel like they're supporting you on a deeper level. On my own newsletter, some people stick with the standard subscription while others spring for a Founding Member tier because they see the long-term payoff. Both groups matter, and help capture different types of subscribers.

Here's why offering two simple tiers is the move: it keeps the barrier low for price-sensitive readers and gives superfans a way to invest in a higher fidelity experience. Win-win.

Picture it like this:

- **Standard Subscription is the essentials.** Your regular posts plus comment access, maybe a community thread.
- **Premium Subscription is everything above plus VIP treatment.** Live classes, bonus essays, subscriber-only Q&As, or behind-the-scenes content. Toss in something scarce like limited coaching slots or a private audio feed, and now you're running a velvet rope situation.

That premium tier is your profit booster. It rewards your most loyal readers and makes them feel like insiders while keeping the base tier accessible to the masses. And don't worry—you don't need to create seventeen new products to justify it. Add what feels sustainable and truly valuable.

Now, let's talk perks. What can make your newsletter feel indispensable?

Here are some ideas:

- **Digital downloads:** templates, checklists, workbooks, or even a bonus chapter tied to your niche.
- **Early access:** give paying members first dibs on new essays or serialized chapters.
- **Exclusive spaces:** private chat threads or a members-only forum where people feel like they've got the keys to the VIP lounge.
- **Subscriber discounts:** partner with brands or tools your audience already uses and make them feel like they're getting inside deals.

Pressure-test every perk before you add it. Ask: would my readers actually use this, or does it just sound fancy? Extra features no one touches are like throw pillows—they look nice in pictures, annoying in real life.

The point is this: you're not pricing your effort. Similar to client work, you're pricing the transformation, the access, and the experience.

When you do that well, $5 a month starts to feel like a steal—and $20 feels like a privilege.

Build Your Audience Engine

If you want subscribers, you need readers first.

This is the step most writers skip. You can't just announce your paid newsletter to the world and expect people to magically appear, credit card in hand. Even the best content needs a way to be found.

Your subscribers will come from many different places: search engines, social media, other newsletters, podcasts, word of mouth. The key is to think of it like building a funnel. And don't get intimidated by the jargon—at its simplest, a funnel is just a path that moves someone from "I've never heard of you" to "I want to pay to read everything you write."

The top of the funnel is anything that catches someone's attention. A free blog post that answers their question. A social post they see shared by a friend. A podcast interview where you talk about your expertise. These pieces introduce you to new readers and get them curious.

Next, you invite them onto your free newsletter or email list. This is crucial. Social media algorithms change. Podcast listeners forget. But when someone signs up for your free newsletter, you own that relationship. You can show up in their inbox week after week, building trust and demonstrating the value you offer.

Once they know you and love your free content, they're much more likely to upgrade to your paid tier. Because now they see you as a trusted voice worth investing in.

Pick one channel to start and master it:

- **SEO-optimized blog posts.** Answer real questions your ideal reader is asking.
- **Daily social posts.** Repurpose your best essays or share behind-the-scenes thinking.
- **Guest interviews or podcast appearances.** Tap into audiences who already want what you offer.
- **Ads.** Only after you know your free content converts, you can dig into paid promotion to amplify what's already working.

Dickens didn't have social media, but he sold serials with posters and word-of-mouth teasers. Same game, bigger megaphone.

Bottom line: marketing your paid newsletter isn't about being salesy. It's about making sure the people who need what you offer can actually find you. Your funnel doesn't have to be fancy, but it does have to exist. Build it deliberately, feed it consistently, and watch it compound over time.

Make Consistency Your Superpower

Predictability is the secret handshake of paid newsletters. When readers hand over their credit card, they're not just buying your words—they're buying the comfort of knowing those words will arrive when you said they would. Consistency builds trust. And trust is what keeps subscriptions renewing like clockwork.

Think of your newsletter like a train schedule. If the 8:05 arrives at 8:05 every week, people build their routines around it. They start looking forward to it, counting on it. If it's late half the time, they stop showing up to the platform. Your readers are the same way. Reliability isn't glamorous, but it's the quiet superpower behind every thriving paid newsletter.

Here's my recommendation: publish at least once a week. If you want to accelerate growth, twice a week is even better. These don't need to be essays that rival *War and Peace*. A sharp 500-word dispatch, a curated list, a single brilliant idea—that's enough to keep readers hooked. The point isn't to overwhelm them. It's to stay top of mind, like a favorite columnist who drops by on schedule.

Of course, showing up regularly is easy in theory, harder when life throws deadlines, drama, and dentist appointments at you. So make it as painless as possible. Start by creating a rhythm that works for you.

I like the weekly cadence because it keeps the content fresh and current. Newsletters work best when they feel alive, like they were written for this moment, not pulled from a dusty folder. But if you're worried about blank-page panic, build an editorial calendar. Knowing what you'll write before you sit down is like keeping breadcrumbs on the trail. It gets you to the finish line faster.

Another trick? Batch content. If you know you'll be traveling or slammed with other work, write a couple of editions ahead. Future You will send you a thank-you card. And as your newsletter grows, don't be afraid to delegate and hire help.

But let's zoom out. Writing on a schedule isn't just about pleasing readers, it's about shaping yourself. A newsletter is a promise you make to them and to you. Every time you hit publish on time, you reinforce your own discipline. That matters because discipline is the highest form of self-respect. It says, "I take my craft seriously." And readers feel that.

There's also a hidden creative bonus here: deadlines make you sharper. Ask any longtime professional writer like a journalist or TV writer. They'll tell you that inspiration is fickle, but discipline delivers. Constraints breed creativity.

When you know a post is due Thursday morning, your brain stops waiting for the muse and starts generating ideas like a caffeinated intern. Over time, this rhythm strengthens your creative muscle until publishing becomes second nature.

So treat your schedule like sacred ground. Put it in your calendar. Guard it from distractions. Because every on-time post isn't just an email—it's a brick in the empire you're building.

Keep Readers Hooked Beyond "Hello"

Getting a new subscriber is like getting a first date. Exciting, full of possibility. But the real magic? Turning that date into a long-term relationship. Because churn—the silent breakup—is the enemy of subscription businesses. Every time someone leaves, it's not just a lost reader. It's lost revenue, lost momentum, and a tiny crack in the empire you're building.

So how do you keep people around? Start by making the experience feel worth it from day one. When someone joins, they should immediately know, *"This was a good decision."* That could mean giving them a quick-win resource or a welcome note that feels warm instead of robotic. If their first impression is an empty inbox and a shrug, they'll wander off before your next billing cycle hits.

Beyond the intro, your best retention strategy is ridiculously simple: deliver consistent value they can't imagine living without. That means watching your quality like a hawk. What posts get opened and shared? Which ones tank? What prompts comments or sparks community buzz? This is where you stop acting like the dreamy artist and start acting like a CEO. You write like an artist, edit like an editor, and then review your stats like a data-obsessed executive. Because the numbers don't lie, and they'll tell you what your readers really want.

Occasional surprises help too. A bonus essay out of nowhere, a replay of a live Q&A, an invite to a private thread just for long-time subscribers—these moments create delight, and delight is sticky.

Community rituals work the same way. Things like weekly "Win Threads" or subscriber-only AMAs give readers a reason to keep showing up beyond your core content. And don't underestimate the power of asking what they want. A simple survey or open-ended prompt like, "What should I tackle next?" signals that their voice matters. People stay where they feel seen.

But here's the truth: none of that matters if the core content gets lazy. A shiny onboarding gift won't compensate for posts that feel phoned in. Retention lives and dies on trust—trust that you'll show up on schedule, that what you deliver will feel fresh, and that the subscription keeps earning its keep in their budget.

So yes, throw in the occasional perk. Build little rituals. But never forget the simplest rule in the retention playbook: keep giving people a reason to stay. The minute they stop feeling like they'd miss you if you disappeared, the unsubscribe button starts calling their name.

Scale Beyond the Newsletter

Think of your newsletter as your launchpad, your control tower, your radio station broadcasting straight into the inboxes of people who actually want to hear from you. When you hit "send," you're deepening trust. And trust is currency.

Here's where it gets exciting: that recurring revenue isn't just padding your bank account, it's buying you options. Your newsletter becomes proof of concept and a portfolio rolled into one.

High end clients who might hire you for a ghostwriting project? They're going to look you up online. And when they land on a thriving newsletter with paying subscribers, that screams authority. It says, "People value my words enough to put a credit card down." That's social proof in its purest form. Your newsletter is also a client funnel, quietly working for you while you sleep. The same list that supports your subscription model can convert into consulting work, speaking jobs, or big-ticket ghostwriting projects.

But we're not stopping there. Your newsletter is a reader funnel, too. It's the bridge to your next book launch. It's how you turn an audience into a preorder army, how you hit bestseller lists without begging a single algorithm for mercy. It's where you nurture super-fans, the ones who will not only buy your book but gift it to friends and quote it at dinner parties. The newsletter is your heartbeat, pumping energy to every limb of your writing empire.

And then comes the real magic: expansion. You can take your best essays and spin them into an online course that sells for $5,000 a seat. You can package your archives into an e-book or a guide and sell it as a digital download. You can host an in-person retreat for premium subscribers who want face time with you, and charge accordingly. You can even strike sponsorship deals with brands your readers already love, turning your newsletter into a revenue-generating bill-board that doesn't feel like an ad.

Here's the secret: all of this grows from the consistent habit of showing up in your readers' inbox with value they can't get anywhere else. Your newsletter is not an extra chore. It's the engine that powers everything: client acquisition, book sales, community building, brand authority. It's your distribution channel. It's your proof of demand. It's your safety net when social media platforms implode for the fifth time this year.

The three pillars in this book—ghostwriting, newsletters, and self-publishing—aren't random tactics tossed together. They're a system. They feed each other. The audience you grow through your newsletter buys your book. The credibility you build through your newsletter lands clients who trust your expertise. And the revenue from your newsletter funds the freedom to keep writing.

If you've ever wondered what a seven-figure writing business looks like, it starts right here—with a paid newsletter as the hub, and everything else orbiting around it like planets.

So no, this isn't diluting your focus. This is stacking your power. A paid newsletter isn't just a nice-to-have. It's your launchpad to becoming a one-person media empire—or, at the very least, the kind of writer who wakes up on a Tuesday, sends an email, and makes thousands of dollars before lunch.

That's the dream. And it's available to you the moment you commit to hitting send.

Power Move: Launch Your Paid Newsletter in 15 Minutes

Ready to stop overthinking and actually get started? Here's your no-excuses template to launch your paid newsletter *today*.

This is how you go from an idea in your head to a live offer in under 15 minutes:

1. **Define Your Promise (3 minutes).** Write a single sentence that tells readers what they'll get and why it matters. Example: "Weekly deep dives into hidden history that help you see today's world more clearly."
2. **Choose Your Two Tiers (4 minutes).** Pick prices that feel fair for the value you're offering. Don't overcomplicate it when creating your two tiers:
   a. Standard Tier. Regular posts, community access.
   b. Premium Tier. Exclusive bonuses like Q&As, resource libraries, or early access.
3. **Sketch Your First Three Issues (4 minutes).** Jot down simple titles or topics. You don't need the full drafts now—just know where you're going.
4. **Name Your Newsletter (2 minutes).** It doesn't have to be perfect. It just has to be memorable enough to make someone click "subscribe."
5. **Commit to a Schedule (2 minutes).** Weekly? Twice per week? Promise what you can actually deliver—and then deliver it like clockwork.

That's it. Now it's time to pick a platform and hit publish. You're live.

You can tweak, polish, and optimize forever, but you can't grow what you don't launch. Get it up. Get it out. Start showing up for your readers today.

Your paid newsletter is not just another project. It's your engine for freedom, ownership, and creative control. Build it like it matters— because it does.

Amy's Field Notes: The Magic Beyond the Money

It was a Wednesday in Buenos Aires when I got the email: "Hey Amy, I saw from your newsletter that you're in Argentina. So am I! Want to grab coffee?"

Just like that, I was running out the door to meet up with a fellow writer and subscriber who had become part of the beating heart of my community. The same thing has happened in Copenhagen. Tokyo. All over the world.

It's one of the wildest, most rewarding things about building my paid newsletters. I thought I was launching an educational product. An information service. What I actually built was a network of incredible humans who care about the craft of writing as much as I do—and who also care about the power of the community we were building together.

Even recently, I found myself dancing around the living room in full celebration mode because one of our paid subscribers at MakeWritingYourJob.com shared that they had just landed their first memoir ghostwriting project through the Writing Job Board. They'd done other types of writing before, but this was their dream niche. They shared their win with me and the community so we could all celebrate together.

Kyle laughed and said, "I hope your subscribers know how psyched you get for them."

And he's right, I'm probably more excited about their wins than my own some days.

That's the real reward. The paid newsletter isn't just a line item on my income statement. It's a living, breathing ecosystem of writers helping writers. Of people making real career moves. Of opportunities that might never have found the right person without this connective tissue between us.

And that's the part I want you to hold onto if you're about to launch your own. It's easy to think of a paid newsletter in purely transactional terms. To see it as a way to "get paid for your writing." And sure, that's part of it. That's the fuel.

But the real power? That's in the transformation you create. The lives you touch. The creative energy you amplify and direct. The doors you hold open for the next person.

When you think about launching your own paid newsletter, try to see it not just as a project but as a calling. That shift in mindset is what infuses your work with the kind of magic that readers feel instantly—and go from being just readers, to true fans and evangelists for what you're building.

This isn't just a business model. It's a way to leave the world a little better than you found it.

11

SELF-PUBLISH LIKE A TYCOON

Brandon Sanderson is one of the most successful fantasy authors alive. Legions of devoted fans. Books translated around the world. You'd think his publisher would treat someone of his status like royalty—red carpets, unlimited marketing budgets, full creative freedom.

But even Sanderson wasn't satisfied. He realized that no matter how many millions his publisher made off him, he was still operating inside their system. Their timelines. Their pricing. Their constraints.

So he went direct. In 2022, he launched a Kickstarter to self-publish special editions of four new books, completely outside the traditional publishing house machinery. The result? Over $41 million was brought in from fans buying his books, making it the most successful publishing Kickstarter in history.[1] Sanderson earned both cold, hard cash *and* control over his distribution. He offered fans custom covers, deluxe editions, and a buying experience designed entirely around them.

---

1. Rollin Bishop, "Brandon Sanderson's Kickstarter Campaign Becomes Most-Funded Publishing Project Ever," *Engadget*, accessed 2025, https://www.engadget.com/brandon-sanderson-kickstarter-campaign-record-most-funded-091530765.html

Or look at Taylor Swift. She didn't just buy back her masters—she re-recorded them to take ownership of her catalog.[2] When she released her Eras Tour concert film, she skipped Hollywood studios and went directly to theaters. Even her tour book? Self-published.[3]

Why? Because control is power.

If Sanderson and Swift, two of the most successful, well-resourced artists alive, are willing to opt out of middlemen and go direct, what does that say to the rest of us?

It says the gatekeepers aren't the prize. Your audience is.

Self-publishing is no longer a fallback or a dirty word. It's the fastest way to own your work, serve your audience, and keep the lion's share of the rewards.

Why You Should Self-Publish

Self-publishing isn't a consolation prize, it's the power move. It's the difference between renting your creative life from a gatekeeper and owning the damn building. Traditional publishing sells you prestige and sprinkles of validation, but behind the curtain? You're signing away control, speed, and a huge chunk of your profits.

As I've mentioned before in this book, when you go traditional publishing, you don't call the shots. You don't choose your title. You don't pick the cover (hope you like "safe and marketable beige"). You don't decide if your book is hardcover, paperback, or both. You don't control your pricing. And if you dream of special editions, box sets, or international availability? Get in line. Your publisher might decide maybe in 18 months. Meanwhile, you're still waiting for an email response about the font size on the back cover.

And the timeline? Traditional publishing moves slower than a

---

2. "Taylor Swift Announces She Bought Back Her Masters with Heartfelt Note to Fans, 'Bursting into Tears,'" *Page Six*, accessed 2025, https://pagesix.com/2025/05/30/ entertainment/taylor-swift-announces-she-bought-back-her-masters-with-heartfelt-note-to-fans-bursting-into-tears/

3. Wikipedia contributors, "The Eras Tour Book," *Wikipedia*, accessed 2025, https://en. wikipedia.org/wiki/The_Eras_Tour_Book

DMV line in a power outage. Two to three years from book deal to bookstore is standard. That's prehistoric compared to self-publishing, where you can go from finished draft to global distribution in weeks —not years.

Here's why self-publishing works so well for authors:

- **Higher Margins that Actually Matter.** Instead of $2.50 per hardcover in royalties, you can earn anywhere from $4-$6 on a paperback and $6-$8 on an e-book—or more, depending on what pricing you choose. That means 10,000 e-book sales could put $80,000 in your pocket, while a traditionally published author could make less than half that for the same sales, depending on their deal and royalty rate.
- **Faster to Market.** Traditional publishing is a two-to-three-year slog from handshake to launch. Self-publishing lets you upload files, approve proofs, and hit "publish" in weeks. You can launch multiple books a year and build momentum while the Big Five are still debating your subtitle.
- **Total Creative Control.** Want a luxe hardcover with sprayed edges? Done. Want a minimalist cover or a bold statement design? Your call. Set your price, run flash sales, bundle your book with a course or newsletter. You are the CEO of your own publishing house.
- **Data Ownership and Audience Insight.** With self-publishing, you see real-time sales data. You know which keywords convert, which ads work, and which readers are buying. Traditional authors? They get quarterly royalty statements formatted like ancient scrolls.
- **Long-Term Equity.** Your reader list is the holy grail. You own it. Forever. That means when you release the next book—or launch a course, a membership, or a retreat— you have a direct line to buyers who already trust you.

That's the difference between one payday and a scalable business.

- **Print-on-Demand = Zero Risk.** No pallets of unsold books collecting dust in your garage. Upload your files to a print-on-demand service and they handle printing, packing, and global shipping. You can offer hardcovers, paperbacks, e-books, and audiobooks without investing in inventory upfront.

Need another example? Hugh Howey's book *Wool* started as a self-published novella. Readers demanded more. He kept serializing, and eventually his book sales topped over $150,000 per *month* from e-book sales alone as an independent author.[4] *Wool* topped bestseller charts, sold over a million copies, was optioned for film and TV, and earned him a higher level of negotiating power than a standard traditionally published author.

He didn't wait for permission. He wrote for his audience, not gatekeepers.

Own Your Book, Own the Business

Every good movement has a manifesto. Every religion has a sacred text.

Your book is that text—for your world, your work, your readership. Whether it's a sweeping fantasy novel or a nonfiction framework for reinvention, your book is more than content. It's canon. It defines your voice, your ideas, your story—and when you self-publish, you control every word of it.

That control is the key to building a business, not just a book.

When you own your rights, you don't just own a manuscript. You own intellectual property. You own the product, the brand, the voice

---

4. Karen Weintraub, "How Hugh Howey Turned His Self-Published Story *Wool* into a Success & a Book Deal," *Writer's Digest*, accessed 2025, https://www.writersdigest.com/be-inspired/how-hugh-howey-turned-his-self-published-story-wool-into-a-success-a-book-deal

—and every downstream revenue stream that flows from it. Traditional publishing carves that up and keeps a majority stake. But in self-publishing? You're the sole license holder of your own universe.

Your book becomes the centerpiece of a much larger creator empire:

- **Courses and Workshops.** Teach your method. Break down your ideas. Build a learning ladder that starts with the book and expands into premium education.
- **Merch and Limited Editions.** From character-inspired candles to custom hardcovers, superfans want physical keepsakes from the worlds you create.
- **Paid Newsletters and Community Spaces.** Invite readers deeper into your orbit—bonus content, behind-the-scenes insights, ongoing storylines, or early peeks at what's coming next.
- **Live Events and VIP Experiences.** Your book gives people a reason to show up. Turn launches into parties. Offer immersive retreats. Build community around your narrative or philosophy.
- **Media and Licensing.** When you control the IP, you control the upside. Pitch directly. Negotiate film and TV rights on your terms. No middlemen skimming half the deal.

A strong book also fuels your newsletter, and vice versa. Readers who trust you with a $10 e-book will often become subscribers, course buyers, merch collectors, even lifelong fans. And that recurring revenue? That's the difference between hoping your book "sells well" and building a long-term income engine.

This is why self-publishing isn't just a format. It's a strategy. A scalable path for authors who want to build something bigger than a single title.

If you treat your book like an asset instead of an end goal, you'll start to see its full potential—as a launchpad, a business model, a legacy.

The 7-Day Book Outline

Want to go from "I have an idea" to a first outline in a single week? Here's your roadmap:

- **Day 1: Define Your Concept.** What's your book in one sentence? Who's it for? If you can't summarize it, you can't sell it.
- **Day 2: Nail the Target Reader.** Who are you helping, entertaining, or transforming? What do they want on page one—and on the last page?
- **Day 3: Spy on the Competition.** List 3–5 of the top books in your niche, and go and read them (or at least parts of them!) if you haven't already. What hooks readers? What gaps can you fill?
- **Day 4: Map the Structure.** Nonfiction: draft your main sections or chapters. Fiction: sketch the big plot arcs or acts.
- **Day 5: Flesh Out the Beats.** Drop 3–5 bullet points per chapter or act. Think turning points, lessons, cliffhangers.
- **Day 6: Hook & Pitch.** Write your elevator pitch in two sentences. Make it irresistible.
- **Day 7: Review & Refine.** Would you buy this book? If not, go back and develop and sharpen the material until you would.

At the end of seven days, you've got a battle plan—not just an idea. Now let's talk about getting that book in readers' hands without feeling like a carnival barker.

The Basics of Writing Your Book and Preparing for Publication

You've got your outline. Great. Now comes the hard part: turning that skeletal plan into something with muscle, skin, and a heartbeat. This stage isn't glamorous. It's not sipping an espresso while your book magically writes itself. It's trench work—but if you stick with it, you'll come out holding a manuscript instead of just good intentions.

Phase One: Write and Edit Like You Mean It

Step One: Draft the Damn Thing

Every masterpiece starts out as a mess. Your only job right now is to produce an ugly first draft. Ugly like "troll under the bridge" ugly. Done beats perfect every single time.

Set a daily word count goal. It doesn't need to be Tolstoy-level. A thousand words per day will add up fast. Pair that with weekly accountability check-ins, ideally with a writer friend or a community that will lovingly drag you if you slack off. Isolation breeds excuses. Community breeds progress.

By the way, no one cares if you wrote those words while perched on a mountaintop or hunched over a sticky diner booth. All that matters is that you hit the keys until your outline transforms into a complete draft.

Step Two: Structural Edit (AKA, Let's See If This Thing Has Bones)

Once you've got a draft, don't rush to pretty it up. First, you need to know if your story—or your nonfiction argument—actually makes sense. That's where a developmental editor comes in. They're like a literary architect: they tell you if the foundation is cracked, if the pacing sags like an old couch, or if your characters have the depth of a kiddie pool.

Yes, you could just ask your cousin who "reads a lot," but a pro editor will catch things amateurs never will. They'll make your book stronger and teach you lessons you'll carry into every project after this. Think of it as paying tuition for your writing degree—except way cheaper and with immediate ROI. If you need help finding one, post a job listing at MakeWritingYourJob.com and let editors come to you at a range of price points.

Step Three: Beta Readers and Line Editing

After you've wrestled your book into better shape structurally, it's time to see how actual humans react. Enter beta readers, who are test pilots for your book. They'll tell you where they got hooked, where they skimmed, and where they wanted to hurl your book across the room. Some authors also use alpha readers, who read earlier drafts, but personally? I skip straight to beta. Your mileage may vary, so consider both and choose your adventure.

Revise based on feedback that makes sense (and ignore the note that says, "can this murder mystery have more dragons?" Unless, of course, that's the book you really want to write).

Next comes the line editor, whose job is to take your sentences to finishing school. Developmental editors fix the blueprint whereas line editors rearrange the furniture and slap your bad habits into shape. They focus on rhythm, flow, and clarity, while also catching typos and inconsistencies. Sometimes they'll even fact-check if your manuscript calls for it. The difference? Developmental edit = big picture. Line edit = zoomed in on every syllable.

Phase Two: Package It Like a Pro

Once your words are polished, it's time to dress them up for the ball. Here's where most beginners cheap out—and regret it.

- **Cover Design.** Hire a professional. A good cover is a sales tool. Your book's outfit is what convinces strangers to take it home. Readers really do judge a book by its cover, so invest accordingly. You can find designers at all price points, but don't settle for the $5 template that screams "amateur." Your future readers—and your bank account—deserve better. There are going to be more and more AI tools that will also generate cover designs for you, and if you decide to use one of these make sure you create a cover design that's aesthetic, not generic.

- **Book Description.** This is your back-cover blurb and your sales pitch rolled into one. Study copywriting basics because this is where conversions happen. Hook the reader with curiosity and clarity. If you're on Amazon or other big platforms, think like a search engine: sprinkle in keywords people actually type when hunting for a book like yours. (Yes, that means doing a little SEO homework.)

- **ISBNs and Imprints.** ISBNs are like your book's Social Security number, and they identify it worldwide. You can buy them at Bowker's website if you're in the U.S. If you're planning a career as an indie author, buy a pack and create your own publishing imprint. It sounds fancy, but really it's just branding and back office management, and it makes you look pro when bookstores are stocking their shelves with your bestsellers.

Phase Three: Proof, Format, and Upload

After line editing, you still need a final proofread. Ideally, hire a different proofreader than your line editor, as they'll spot things fresh eyes can catch. Once that's locked, move on to interior design and formatting. Your book needs to look polished on both Kindle screens and in print. You can DIY with book formatting tools, or hire someone who eats EPUB files for breakfast.

Finally, upload your files to print-on-demand platforms like Amazon KDP or IngramSpark. These services are your global warehouse: no inventory risk, no boxes in your garage. Click upload, set your price, and let the algorithms do their thing once you've got a book marketing plan in place. Each platform has its quirks, so expect a learning curve, or outsource to someone who already speaks fluent self-publishing.

Once you've got your material prepared for upload, it's time to dive into the art of book marketing.

Book Marketing Without Begging

Minutes before writing this section, I hung up from a strategy call with my book marketer and publicist. We weren't just mapping dates or drafting ad copy. We were dissecting the book launch we're working on as an art project. Talking angles, storylines, stats, incentives, and how to make sure the marketing doesn't feel like a used car salesman screaming "buy now," but like a conversation readers want to join.

Because here's the truth most writers won't say out loud: marketing often feels like begging. Like standing on the street corner waving your book around. "Please notice me. Please buy." And for many of us—especially the ones who see our writing as personal or even sacred—that feels gross.

But good marketing isn't begging. It's helping someone solve a problem they actually want solved. Done right, marketing is a service that connects readers to the books they'll love the most. It's creative. It's storytelling layered on top of your craft. You're not tricking anyone. You're clarifying, and making the path from need to solution easy and irresistible.

That's what we were plotting on that call. How to make sure this book's marketing is fun, natural, and artistic in its own right. How to use narrative, design, and authenticity to earn attention instead of demand it.

Because if you treat marketing as a separate, lesser afterthought —a necessary evil tacked on to the "real" work—your masterpiece will die in a digital warehouse. But if you treat it as the second canvas, the conversation your work sparks in the world, it becomes an extension of your craft.

Yes, there's data to track. Yes, there are emails and landing pages and conversion rates. But underneath all of that is an invitation: *Come see what I made for you.*

If the thought of "selling" makes your soul itch, remember: traditional publishers would make you do this work anyway, and keep most of your money in the process. When you self-publish, every ounce of effort compounds in your own bank account, not someone else's.

So let's map a launch plan that sells without sleaze, and gives you the best shot at bestseller lists without sacrificing your sanity.

Launch Like a List-Topper

Let's get real: you don't need to hit *The New York Times* or Amazon bestseller charts for your book to be a success. You can make six figures in sales without ever hitting any of those lists.

But let's also be honest, there are reasons you might want to aim for those lists. Those little badges aren't real power. They don't make you a better writer or automatically sell your next book. But they are social proof.

A bestseller label opens doors. It can help you land podcast interviews, speaking gigs, consulting clients, or ghostwriting work. It signals that you know how to deliver something people want. It gives your readers and clients a reason to trust you.

In other words, it's not the power itself. But it can amplify your power. That's why this next section will show you how to approach your book launch like a three-month campaign designed to maximize sales velocity and give you the best shot at hitting the NYT bestseller list or Amazon charts—even as an indie author.

Because here's the truth: self-published books can and do make these lists. Robert Kiyosaki's *Rich Dad, Poor Dad* was self-published before hitting the NYT list. But it didn't get there by accident. It made enough noise that the NYT couldn't ignore it—even though they famously turn their noses up at self-published books. In fact, *The New York Times* list is editorial, not purely sales-based. There's no guaranteed formula to get on. But if you sell enough books, fast enough, across enough retailers, you make it very hard for them to exclude you.

Countless indie romance authors have also hit these major lists. Take Callie Hart, for example. She self-published her romantasy novel *Quicksilver*, which not only became a #1 *New York Times* bestseller, but also landed her a seven-figure Netflix deal for the screen adaptation.

If you make enough noise, they have to pay attention.

That's the game. You're not throwing a polite garden party. You're launching a blockbuster.

Bottom line? A bestseller list isn't magic. It's a combination of a great draft and a marketing plan. But even if you have a great marketing plan and sell thousands of copies, a bestseller list placement isn't guaranteed.

Case Study: Alex Hormozi's $100M Money Models as a Live-Launch Masterclass

Alex Hormozi didn't just release a book, he launched a full-blown broadcast event designed to break records.

On August 16, 2025, Hormozi went live for a marathon nine-and-a-half-hour livestream, turning what could've been a simple launch day for his book *$100M Money Models* into a cross between a TED Talk, a webinar on steroids, and a hype rally for business nerds. No countdown timers. No pretense. Just Hormozi on camera, selling the hell out of his book—and doing it in a way that made his audience feel like they were part of something big. Something built for them.

By the end of the day, *$100M Money Models* had smashed the Guinness World Record for fastest-selling nonfiction book, with over 2.97 million copies sold in 24 hours. That's a strategic detonation of what a book launch can do when it's engineered like a campaign and not just a post.

Now, full disclosure: depending on your corner of the internet, Alex Hormozi might come across as a hustle bro in a muscle tank top yelling about CAC and EBITDA. And look, he knows. He's not trying to be your soft-spoken writing coach. He's speaking directly to entre-preneurs, business builders, and the specific subset of Type-A systems junkies who are already bought in. If you're not in the Hormoziverse, his tone might feel aggressive or over-the-top. But if you *are* his audience? It hits like gospel.

And that's kind of the point. Hormozi doesn't dilute his messaging to appeal to everyone. He tailors it for the people who want what he's selling, and he shows up *hard* for those people. His launch was a value stack for his people: books, bonuses, AI tools, live Q&A, and the promise of ongoing business insights. People didn't just buy a book. They bought access. They bought into a system. That's why the numbers were what they were.

Love him or roll your eyes at him, but you can't ignore him. And frankly, I've stolen a few of his strategies myself. Some of his business frameworks have worked wonders in my own work, especially around offer positioning and conversion strategy. You don't have to agree with someone's entire philosophy to learn something useful from them. And in a world where most book launches fizzle out in a week, Hormozi's launch was a reminder that when you treat a book like a business asset—not just a piece of content—it can become a catalytic event.

Now, not every author needs (or wants) to pull off a multimillion-dollar book launch. Plenty of great books build momentum over time. But one truth remains: the more intentional you are about your launch, the less heavy lifting you'll have to do afterward. And whether you're writing for CEOs or romantasy readers, that kind of momentum is worth studying.

Your 90-Day Countdown Campaign

So what does it take?

A big launch isn't something you wake up and decide to do on release day. It's a carefully orchestrated, multi-month campaign designed to build anticipation, stack preorders, and drive a massive week-one sales spike.

Here's how to think about it: you're not just selling a book. You're telling a story about why this book matters, building an audience that cares, and giving them reasons to buy now—not "someday."

Below is a 90-day framework to make that happen:

90-60 Days Before Launch: Plant the Seeds

This is where you reveal the book title, show off the cover, and start telling the story behind the book.

- Share cover reveals in your newsletter and on social media.
- Tell the personal reason you wrote this book.
- Invite early readers into a private launch team or street team group.
- Open preorders on every major retailer.

Important note: bestseller lists count all preorders that ship in the same week of your launch toward that week's sales total. So getting people to preorder early is crucial for list math.

You're setting the stage, building hype, and locking in early sales that will all count when it matters.

Crafting Pre-Order Incentives That Work

Pre-order incentives are tools to get readers to commit early. Think of them as a thank-you that also helps you stack those crucial first-week sales.

These incentives could include:

- Exclusive bonus chapters or early access scenes.
- Printable PDFs like workbooks, discussion guides, or collector dust jackets.
- Private live events or readings for pre-order customers.

Important note: Don't offer incentives in exchange for reviews. Retailers like Amazon prohibit "review incentives" like gift cards or free products specifically for a positive review. You can encourage reviews, but you can't pay for them.

Instead, use pre-order incentives to reward purchasing, not reviewing.

59-30 Days Before Launch: Advance Copies and Blurbs

Now you shift from hype-building to validation.

- Send digital or print ARCs (advance reader copies) to 100–150 reviewers—or more if you can swing it.
- Ask for honest, thoughtful feedback, and time your reviews to drop on launch week.
- Collect blurbs from other authors in your genre or from respected voices your audience knows.

You're stacking social proof and giving readers reasons to trust you before they ever see page one.

29-8 Days Before Launch: Mobilize Your Street Team

Your street team is your secret weapon.

These are your most loyal fans and supporters. They're the people willing to share your book with their networks because they believe in you. Your street team is more than just a mailing list segment. It's your core evangelist group.

They get early access, exclusive content, and the feeling of being insiders. In return, they help spread the word authentically.

Imagine them posting unboxing photos, sharing their favorite lines, leaving early book reviews, or filming quick social videos about why they're excited.

Offline, they might wear "book ambassador" badges at your signings or host small launch parties.

You don't need thousands. Just dozens of committed, excited fans can move the needle.

Your job is to make them feel seen, valued, and part of something bigger than just buying a book.

During this phase:

- Create a private chat, message board, or email thread just for them.
- Give them graphics, quote cards, and sample chapters to share.
- Run weekly challenges to keep them engaged (like posting an unboxing photo or sharing their favorite line).
- Reward them with behind-the-scenes Q&As, sneak peeks, or even signed copies.

Your goal? Turn your readers into your marketers. Make them feel like insiders with a mission.

Think of it like this: big publishers have sales reps and bookstore chains. Indie authors have readers with smartphones and passion.

7-0 Days Before Launch: Seize Launch Week

This is it—the main event.

Your mission is to keep the momentum rolling every single day.

- Host daily live chats or Q&As on platforms your audience uses.
- Post short video teasers, dramatic readings, or blurbs from early reviews.
- Email your list with clear calls to action: "Buy it now."
- Monitor sales dashboards to keep an eye on your rank and see if you need to amplify with targeted ads.

Launch week isn't about one big blast. It's about sustained, relentless attention.

1-21 Days After Launch: Riding the Momentum

The first few days after launch might've felt like a sprint, but the real race starts here. This is the window where momentum can compound or quietly collapse. You've planted the seeds with preorders, early readers, and your street team. Now it's time to fan the flames. The 1-3 week mark is when second-wave opportunities bloom: podcast bookings, newsletter interviews, rankings screenshots, glowing reviews, and organic reader buzz.

- Lock in second-wave media coverage: podcasts, long-form interviews, guest newsletters.
- Share social proof: screenshots of rankings, reviews, reader reactions.
- Encourage your street team to keep posting and celebrating.
- Offer corporate bulk deals after list placements lock, avoiding the bulk-buy warning signs.

Momentum breeds more momentum.

After the Launch: Keep Selling, Keep Learning

Your launch isn't the finish line. It's the starting gun for long-term sales.

Take time to analyze:

- Which channels converted best?
- Which emails or posts drove real sales?
- Which partnerships delivered?

Refine your approach for the next book.

Remember, every new book you launch doesn't just sell itself. It also sells your other books. Readers who love this one will go back and buy the others.

That's the power of building your own backlist.

Why Email Beats Algorithms Every Time in Book Marketing

When I first launched my book *Six-Figure Freelance Writer*, I didn't have a real plan. I thought marketing would be easy because I had 48,000 TikTok followers who loved my freelance writing tips. Surely if even a tiny fraction bought the book, I'd be golden.

Spoiler: that didn't happen.

My videos reached tons of people, but not the right people, and not consistently. Meanwhile, I had only 500 newsletter subscribers at the time. But they were the ones who actually bought the book. When the first sales reports rolled in, it was obvious my newsletter had pulled the heavy weight—not social media.

That was my first real lesson: social media is not sales. *Email* is sales. Even now, after building a bigger audience, my newsletter remains the single most reliable way to launch anything.

Because you own it. Algorithms can't throttle it. Platforms can't ban you. It's your direct line to the people who actually care.

Here's the truth most creators eventually learn the hard way: social media is a rented billboard. Email is the deed to your own shop.

Your post on social media might go viral once. But social doesn't guarantee that your followers see your next post. Or the one after that. Or your book launch announcement at all.

I've said it before in this book, but it's so important I'm saying it to you again: email lands in the inbox. *Every. Time.* Which is why email will always be king.

The Mere-Exposure Edge

People rarely buy the first time they hear your name. Social psychologists call this the "mere-exposure effect": the more often someone encounters you, the more they trust you.[5]

Think about it: if you pop up once in someone's feed, they might smile, even like it. But they'll forget you in two seconds. Show up every week in their inbox with something useful or entertaining? You become a part of their routine. You stop being a stranger. You become their go-to.

That's why consistency matters so much. A weekly newsletter compounds trust in a way even viral social posts can't touch. Your writing becomes familiar. And familiarity sells.

Stop Fearing "Too Much Content"

One of the biggest fears I hear from writers launching books: "Won't people get sick of me?"

Honestly? It's hard to even reach them once.

Most people won't see everything you post, no matter how often you post it. Social feeds are crowded. Inboxes are busy. People forget.

Showing up more than you think you "should" is usually the only way you'll be seen enough to stick. If engagement drops? Don't vanish. Experiment. Tweak your approach. But stay present.

People don't unsubscribe because you're consistent. They unsubscribe because you're boring or irrelevant. Choose consistent.

Power Move: The Clarity Compass

Before you start stacking ISBNs and plotting preorder bonuses, take a breath. The fastest way to sabotage your author career is to sprint toward someone else's dream. Writing a book just because "it sells" without asking if it's yours is how you end up burned out as a writer.

Here's the truth: your book is your flag in the ground. It's what readers will quote when you're not in the room. It's the story—or the system—that will outlive the algorithm spike. So make it count.

---

5. Wikipedia contributors, "Mere-Exposure Effect," *Wikipedia*, accessed 2025, https://en.wikipedia.org/wiki/Mere-exposure_effect

Before moving forward with anything else on your plate today, do this exercise:

The Clarity Journal Session

Give yourself 30 minutes today. Shut the door. Silence the pings. Pull out a notebook or open a blank doc. This isn't about branding or being "marketable." This is about getting radically honest before you hit publish.

Write freely, like nobody will ever read this (because they won't):

1. What do I want to be known for as a writer? When someone says my name, what ideas or feelings do I want to trigger?
2. Which stories or messages won't leave me alone? The ones that hit you in the shower or at a stoplight? They're signals. Follow them.
3. What am I terrified to write—but aching to? Fear is usually pointing toward something real and electric.
4. Am I fiction, nonfiction, or both? Do I want to build worlds from scratch—or decode the one I'm living in? (Hybrid rebels welcome.)
5. If this were the only book I ever wrote, would I still write it? If yes, you're on the right track. If no, what's the book that earns that answer?

Your only rule? Be brutally honest. Say the quiet stuff on paper. Because here's the thing: clarity is leverage. A book born from what lights you up will outlast every trend, every algorithm tweak, every comparison spiral.

Write what makes your pulse race. The market can wait—your voice can't.

Amy's Field Notes: Fast Beats Perfect, Even for Masterpieces

I met an author in Portugal who was deep in the trenches of writing a book proposal. Over dinner on the beach, they described how the proposal alone would likely take a year. They had an agent waiting and giving them notes on their concept. Maybe, if everything went perfectly, the book would see the inside of a bookstore in three or four years.

Meanwhile, I'd just started writing *The Ash Trials*, the first book in my romantasy series. Six months later, when I saw this writer again, *The Ash Trials* was already on shelves. My inbox was full of kind notes from readers. Book influencers were sharing videos and generous reviews. Sales were steady. People were emailing me begging me for the date when the sequel would drop.

And that's the thing no one can take away from me. I didn't wait for someone in an office to decide my words were "marketable." I just published. And the book became real. Tangible. Loved. Earning.

That other author was still in limbo—perfecting the proposal for a book that might never move forward, or if it does, might not exist in readers' hands for years.

The lesson isn't that traditional publishing isn't just broken, it's also slow. And for fiction especially, speed can be your secret weapon.

Because I'm a different person today than I was a year ago. What I care about evolves. What I'm obsessed with shifts. And with fiction, you need to capture that lightning-in-a-bottle moment—the fresh idea that hits you in the gut, the emotional undercurrent you're feeling now. That's the magic. That's what readers respond to.

And you don't need to be perfect to share it.

My favorite example? J.R.R. Tolkien literally revised *The Lord of the Rings* after it was published, changing major details about the ring itself in later editions. After finishing The Lord of the Rings, Tolkien went back and overhauled Chapter 5 of The Hobbit—in the 1951 second edition—turning Gollum from a relatively gracious figure into a murderous, Ring-obsessed presence, ensuring the earlier book aligned more closely with the darker mythology of his later work[OBJ].[6] Later, in 1965, he polished The Lord of the Rings for its second edition —making textual corrections, tightening the timeline, refining Elvish names, and writing a new, forthright Foreword to legitimize the U.S. edition and clarify changes, which is proof that even masterpieces remain editable, so your self-published novel can be, too[OBJ].[7]

That's the freedom of our modern era of self-publishing. If you spot a typo, you don't have to call a printer and pay for reams of new paperbacks. You update the file and re-upload it. Done. Readers who got the original? They have a quirky "first edition." Everyone else gets the fix.

I work with line editors and proofreaders, of course, and I recommend you do, too. I try to put my best foot forward with every book. But perfection isn't the goal—connection is.

Fast beats perfect because published beats invisible. No one can read the story trapped in your head or collecting dust on your desktop.

And timing matters. When I released *The Ash Trials,* romantasy was having a moment. I was devouring those books myself. That energy was real for me, and for readers. Publishing fast let me ride the wave while the zeitgeist was hot. It let me find my true fans who wanted exactly that kind of emotional, magical storytelling *now*.

That's the real power of self-publishing in the digital age. Speed isn't a shortcut. It's a strategy. It lets you seize cultural moments, test ideas in real time, and grow with your readers.

So no, speed publishing isn't sloppy or amateur. It's a new staple of the modern era.

You still do the work. You still care about quality. But you move. You hit publish. You connect.

Because in the end, no one remembers the perfect draft that

---

6. Wikipedia contributors, "A Tolkien Compass," *Wikipedia*, accessed 2025, https://en. wikipedia.org/wiki/A_Tolkien_Compass

7. *Tolkien Gateway*, "The Lord of the Rings Foreword," accessed 2025, https://tolkien gateway.net/wiki/The_Lord_of_the_Rings_Foreword

never left your laptop. They remember the book they held in their hands, the one that made them feel something.

12

YOUR ROADMAP FROM ZERO TO SEVEN-FIGURE WRITER IN 12 MONTHS

When I started taking my writing business seriously, I thought hitting big revenue goals was about one thing: more *time*. More hours. More projects stacked on top of each other until I could see 7-figures in my bank account.

I was wrong.

What actually moved the needle wasn't working more. It was working differently. It was choosing exactly what to sell, pricing it with confidence, building a process that delivered every time, and showing up for the right audience.

This chapter is your roadmap to make that leap from "I guess I'm freelancing" to building an interconnected writing business that has the potential to generate a million dollars in twelve months. I'm going to pull together everything you've read so far in Part Two into an actionable plan, checklist and all.

You don't need perfect prose or a fancy degree. There are tools now that can check your grammar for you. What you do need is an entrepreneurial mindset, an artist's heart, and the discipline to show up. All things we've covered in Part Two, but now we're putting everything together to build your next steps.

I want you to see this chapter as your plan. Your invitation to begin. Your challenge. Because when you know exactly what to do month by month, you can stop asking "Will this work?" and start making it inevitable.

Is 12 Months a Realistic Timeline?

Here's the thing about "realistic": your brain decides what qualifies. If you believe seven figures in a year is delusional, your mind will quietly compile evidence to prove itself right. If you believe it's possible, the same neural machinery flips into GPS mode, scanning for shortcuts, signaling opportunities, nudging you toward the coordinates you've set.

When I first started freelancing, my definition of "realistic" was embarrassingly small. I thought writers only made six figures if they landed a TV staff job or a fat book advance. Everyone I admired wore that same belief like a badge, so I wore it too. That script kept me undercharging and juggling side hustles far longer than necessary. It took a total career plot twist to realize I'd been playing in the wrong sandbox.

I didn't climb straight from zero to seven figures in a year. It took me a decade of trial and error to decode the systems you're about to inherit.

Is it possible for you to make a million in 12 months? Yes, if you stop doubting yourself and start executing like your calendar is a countdown clock. I've watched members of my MakeWritingYour-Job.com community pull off stunts that to outsiders sound like fairy tales: replacing a corporate salary in three months, clearing six figures in five, stacking premium retainers before their first anniversary as a freelancer. The landscape favors speed now. Video calls, remote workflows, and a global client pool were novelties when I began my freelancing career nearly a decade ago. Today, they're the default. Companies understand the ROI of expert freelancers. Decision cycles are measured in hours, not quarters.

Is this audacious goal guaranteed? No. Nothing is. But aiming for seven figures in 12 months—even if you land at $400,000 or $600,000

—is a hell of a lot better than shrinking to "reasonable" and topping out at $100 because you thought dreaming bigger was tacky. Big goals recalibrate your instincts. They make you resourceful. They turn your business into a game you can actually win.

And yes, a little delusion helps. The playful kind that makes you laugh as you write "$1,000,000" on a sticky note and slap it above your monitor. When you gamify the goal, you strip out the panic and keep the creative spark alive. You stop thinking like a starving artist and start moving like a strategist.

So is a seven-figure year realistic? That's the wrong question.

The real question is: are you willing to think and act like it is? Because the moment you do, you'll notice something wild—your brain starts hunting for ways to make it true. That's when this roadmap stops being a thought experiment and starts being a race you can actually run.

The 3 Essential Pillars

If you want this roadmap to work not just as a dream vision board but as a bank statement, you have to master three things in parallel: craft, strategy, and audience. These aren't optional electives. They're the load-bearing walls of your writing empire. Knock one out, and the whole structure buckles.

Before we dive into the tactical month-by-month play, let's talk about these pillars in real life—not as inspirational quotes but as the messy, misunderstood, and ultimately liberating truths that make or break your seven-figure year.

1. Craft: The Myth of Perfect and the Power of Done

Let's get one thing straight: you do not need to be the next Shakespeare to clear seven figures. What you do need is the ability to deliver words that do something: solve a problem, spark a feeling, move a human being from point A to inspired.

Most writers think craft is a bouncer at the VIP door, checking

MFA degrees and Oxford commas. Not true. Craft is a muscle, and like every muscle, it responds to reps. Not wishful thinking, not "someday I'll take a masterclass." Real reps. The more you write, the sharper you get. The people making real money aren't obsessing over whether their semicolons look smug. They're shipping drafts, learning on the job, and iterating fast.

Here's the liberating part: you will never be "done" learning craft. Neither will I. Neither will any of the writers you worship. That's the fun of the game. Your writing life will be an endless scavenger hunt: hitting a block, grabbing a craft book or a video breakdown, applying what you need, and moving on. That's how I learned more in a single year of ghostwriting memoirs than I did in my entire USC screen-writing degree.

Craft is not about hoarding theory like a doomsday prepper: you *can* overdose on pure craft philosophy. If you find yourself being overly obsessive about learning the skill of writing, you may be finding a new clever way to procrastinate. Momentum is about building the reflex to keep learning while shipping work. Learn while doing: write the thing. Hit a wall. Diagnose. Level up. Repeat. That loop will carry you further than any professor's red pen ever could.

2. Strategy: The Engine Behind the Curtain

If craft is the art, strategy is the architecture. It's how you decide what to write, how to price it, and how to keep the whole operation from devouring your life force. This book is obsessed with strategy for a reason: without it, you end up in the freelance equivalent of Groundhog Day, hustling for random gigs, nickel-and-dimed by clients who "don't have the budget" but mysteriously find money for that $40,000 brand video they work on with another freelancer.

Strategy is why this roadmap exists. It's why we're about to dive into detailed playbooks for luxury ghostwriting, paid newsletters, and self-publishing empires. Think of it as two halves: macro strategy (big-picture business model, audience positioning, revenue streams) and micro strategy (the nitty-gritty of onboarding calls, proposal templates, pricing scripts). Both matter. Both determine whether you're running a high-ticket writing business or burning out in content-mill purgatory. You already know this, though, as strategy has been the name of the game for everything you've read so far in Part Two.

3. Audience: The Crowd That Crowns You

Money moves when people move toward you, and they only move when they know, like, and trust you. That's your audience. Whether you want to sell books, land six- and seven-figure ghostwriting deals, or build a bestselling paid newsletter, you need humans willing to bet on your ideas and your taste.

But here's the plot twist: your audience often doesn't know what they actually want until you show them. Your job isn't just to give them what they asked for—it's to surprise and delight them with something they didn't even know was possible. That's why building an audience isn't about chasing trends. It's about showing up consistently, sharing your perspective, and delivering value until their loyalty compounds into revenue.

And yes, we've already covered many of the mechanics in Part Two, but the core concept here bears repeating. Without readers and clients, even the best-crafted words die in the dark.

The Imperfect, Inevitable Truth

Here's the caveat: you will not master the three pillars of craft, strategy, and audience all at once. Perfectionism is the assassin of progress. You'll wobble. Some weeks your writing will feel like wizardry but your strategy will be duct tape. Other weeks you'll obsess over marketing and let your written world coast on autopilot. That's okay. The goal here is simply forward motion.

Everything in this roadmap loops back to these three pillars. They're the frame you'll keep reinforcing as you scale from your first invoice to your first million. Nail them imperfectly, and you'll still win. Ignore them, and the ceiling hits hard and early.

So take a breath. Read that last paragraph again. This isn't about flawless execution—it's about relentless iteration. Learn, adjust, move. That's the game.

And the game starts now.

Months 0-3: Lay the Foundation and Earn Your First Income

Your first three months are about proving this is real—not to the world, but to yourself. This stage is less about perfection and more about momentum. You're laying the foundation while sprinting out of the gate: building habits that will compound for years and shipping work before your inner critic has time to stage a coup. Think of it as a double mandate: start writing, start earning.

That means showing up every day to write—even 500 words counts—and publishing before you feel "ready." It means reading one book a week in your niche so your taste sharpens as fast as your skill. It means tossing up a simple portfolio that says, "Here's what I do," and firing off pitches until your first two clients say yes. The work doesn't have to be flawless, but it has to exist in the world, because feedback only arrives after you hit send.

And while you're planting those first revenue seeds, you're also starting your audience engine. Launch your newsletter on Day One. Don't overcomplicate it. Five subscribers or fifty—doesn't matter. Write like someone's listening, because soon they will be. Turn on paid subscriptions now, even if you keep everything outside the paywall at first. You're building the muscle of publishing, the rhythm of showing up, and the trust that will become currency later.

On the back burner? Begin sketching ideas for the book that will make you undeniable. No pressure, no deadlines—just start noodling on ideas and dropping voice notes into your phone. Your book will be your ultimate authority play, the thing that turns you from "freelancer" into "expert."

This chapter gives you the checklist, but the mindset is simple: act before you feel ready. Perfectionism is just procrastination wearing Prada. Your job now is to write, pitch, publish, and keep going until the scoreboard reads $50,000 in cumulative revenue. Do it before your 9-to-5 job if you have to. Three focused hours a day is enough to build a new life while the old one still pays the bills. The clock starts now.

Keep Doing From Day One

- **Write Every Day.** Even 500 words counts. Consistency beats brilliance right now. Build the habit that compounds.
- **Read Like It Pays (Because It Does).** One book a week in your genre or niche. Study structure, voice, and rhythm. Steal what works, remix it into your own style.
- **Build a Simple Portfolio.** One clean page with your offer and 2–3 strong samples. No bells, no whistles—just proof you can deliver.
- **Pitch Relentlessly.** Even though your portfolio may not be rock solid and your social proof a bit light, pitch as if you're a grizzled expert or industry veteran. Reach out to local businesses, old colleagues, or apply to writing jobs on MakeWritingYourJob.com. Goal: land your first two paying clients. Don't quit pitching until you do. Raise your rates with each successful pitch.
- **Set Your $50,000 Target.** Use the pricing strategies that I've discussed in Part Two to structure offers that make that number possible in three months.
- **Play Daily.** Keep the joy alive. Write a poem, a scene, a nonsense list—anything that reminds you why you started. Client work pays the bills, but play keeps you sane.
- **Launch Your Paid Newsletter.** Post 1-2 times per week

from day one. Share value, insights, and behind-the-scenes updates. You're building trust and planting seeds.

- **Start Your Book Blueprint.** Jot ideas, make voice memos, scribble outlines. Your future authority hinges on this project. No pressure, just clarity: what problem do you solve? What transformation do you promise? Or, if your passion lies in the fiction space: what genre are you most excited about? What types of stories do you want to tell?
- **Launch Your Website.** This could be simply one page hosted on an easy website builder with your name and a place for people to sign up for your paid newsletter. As you start launching your freelance writing offerings, include pages with your offer and a place for clients to download your portfolio PDF.
- **Test Your Marketing Channels.** Post on social media, draft your first blog on your website, or experiment with short-form video. Don't aim for viral, aim for visibility.

Mindset checkpoint: Act before you feel ready. Don't let perfectionism sabotage you.

Income goal: $50,000 cumulative revenue. First high-ticket projects sold, first audience members onboarded.

Months 4-6: Define and Sell Your Signature Offer

Welcome to month four! Now it's time to stop being a lamp and start becoming a laser. These next three months are about focus and channeling all that early momentum into a signature offer, scaling your income, and locking in systems that set you up for the big leagues.

Here's the mindset shift: in Months 0-3, you said yes to almost everything because speed mattered more than specificity. Now you get picky. You've tested the waters. You know what work felt good, what clients paid well, and what projects drained your soul faster than a corporate all-hands meeting. This is where you pick your lane, and own it.

That means turning your early experiments into a signature, outcome-driven offer. For some readers of this book, that's a luxury ghostwriting package, but for others maybe it's a retainer for thought-leadership content, a fractional CMO-style writing role, or a premium book editing service. Whatever your signature offer is, you'll define it clearly, price it confidently, and pitch it relentlessly. Return to the ghostwriting chapter if you're still unsure what your offer is.

And here's the kicker: this is usually when writers can ditch their 9-to-5. If you hit your $50,000 revenue goal in the first three months, the math is on your side. Quitting means the hours you spent at the office job you hated can now be shifted so that you can fund your own projects, like drafting your book manuscript. That book will become a trust signal, a client magnet, and a credibility asset that can spin into speaking jobs, partnerships, and media hits. Or maybe it's a fiction book that speaks to your heart. Whatever the book is, that writing work starts now.

At the same time, your newsletter graduates from "nice to have" to "non-negotiable growth engine." You've spent three months publishing and learning what resonates. Now it's time to refine your voice, double down on what performs, and start nudging readers into your paid tier. This audience will bankroll your next chapter—literally.

The rule for this phase: say no to the wrong work so you can scale the right work. Fewer, higher-paying clients. Stronger audience plays. Everything you do now sets up the compounding effect that turns six figures into seven.

Keep Doing

- **Daily Writing Habit.** Keep hitting that 500+ word goal, even on client-heavy days.
- **Newsletter Cadence.** Continue posting 1-2 times per week. Consistency drives trust.

- **Pitching Discipline.** If you're not fully booked at your new rates, keep sending pitches every day and applying to more freelance writing jobs. Cold outreach will drive your freelance writing career so you can create more competition amongst your current clients and drive up your rates.

New for Months 4-6

- **Define Your Signature Offer.** Review what you've done, what paid best, and what you loved. Package this into one premium, outcome-focused service.
- **Launch High-End Ghostwriting (or Equivalent).**
  - Write a clear deliverable list.
  - Price for transformation, not hours.
  - Map your client journey: onboarding → drafting → white-glove delivery → final wrap.
- **Raise Your Price Floor.** Eliminate low-paying work. Every "yes" must move you closer to $250,000 cumulative revenue by the end of month 6.
  - Pitch Bigger: Start targeting marquee clients. Tap into referrals, social media, private masterminds, and investor networks where premium buyers hang out.
- **Scale Your Paid Newsletter.**
  - Analyze which posts resonated most in Months 0-3.
  - Create similar high-value pieces to attract paid subscribers.
  - Experiment with light paywalls for bonus content, behind-the-scenes updates, or Q&As.
- **Draft Your Book Manuscript.**
  - Use the outline you started earlier as your roadmap.
  - Block weekly writing sprints and treat this like a client deliverable.

- Share snippets with your audience to build anticipation (and future buyers).
- **Continue to Play With Marketing Channels.** Ramp up your visibility beyond pitching. Create your alchemy of social media posts, blog content, short-form videos. Don't aim for viral: aim for steady visibility that builds your brand and funnels readers into your newsletter, and eventually to your book.
- **Optimize Your Systems.** Start building templates for proposals, client onboarding, and revision workflows so you can scale without burning out.

Mindset checkpoint: Saying no creates space for the work that multiplies your impact.

Income goal: $250,000 cumulative revenue by end of Month 6. Signature offer fully booked. Paid newsletter tier active. Draft in motion.

Months 7-9: Systematize and Build Your Audience

You've got proof of concept. You've booked premium clients. Your newsletter is now an engine. These next three months are about professional polish and precision. This is where you go from "freelancer with hustle" to "writer with a brand."

Why now? Because momentum without systems becomes chaos, and chaos kills creativity. By this stage, you should have real revenue and early audience traction. Now you need to protect your time, scale what works, and refine your identity so you look as premium as you charge. That means tightening your operations, leveling up your visual branding, and building the infrastructure for your biggest marketing move yet: your book launch.

Think of this phase as creating gravity. You're pulling people into a cohesive brand experience—your website, your newsletter, your social presence—all aligned, all pointing toward your signature offers and your upcoming book. You're not just a service provider anymore.

You're becoming a thought leader with assets that can out-earn you while you sleep.

The mindset shift here: consistency becomes your moat. Systems keep you sane, branding amplifies your authority, and preparation prevents a sloppy book rollout that wastes months of hard work. This is the quarter where you stop blending in and start broadcasting who you are, and why people should trust you with their time, attention, and wallets.

Keep Doing

- **Write Daily.** Stay loyal to your 500+ words per day.
- **Newsletter Rhythm.** Keep publishing 1-2 times per week. Consistency builds trust and drives conversions.
- **Pitch at Premium.** If you're not fully booked at your new high-ticket rates, keep outreach flowing. Every pitch should aim at dream clients.
- **Paid Newsletter Growth.** Double down on what resonated in Months 4-6. Use analytics to inform your next batch of content.

New for Months 7-9

- **Systematize Everything:**
  - Templates for proposals, contracts, onboarding emails, revision cycles—anything you repeat should now be plug-and-play.
  - Set up project management tools or workflows if you haven't already.
- **Revamp Your Brand:**
  - Hire a pro web designer or invest in a premium template. Your site should feel as upscale as your pricing.
  - Lock in brand assets: fonts, colors, photo style.

- Book a writer photoshoot for professional headshots and lifestyle shots. Your future media kit starts here.
- **Audit and Optimize Funnels:**
  - Which channels drove the most newsletter sign-ups in Months 0-6?
  - Double down on those and cut what's not converting.
  - Create a clear path from social → newsletter → paid tier → book pre-orders.
- **Prep for Your Book Launch:**
  - Finalize your manuscript draft and hand it off to a developmental or line editor.
  - Begin brainstorming cover design and title concepts.
  - Build a launch timeline: ARC (advance reader copy) distribution, influencer outreach, preorder bonuses, and ad strategy.
  - Start teasing your book in your newsletter and social posts to build anticipation.
- **Grow Your Audience Beyond Organic:**
  - Experiment with small paid ads targeting your ideal readers and newsletter subscribers.
  - Join or host virtual events, podcasts, and live streams to widen reach.

Mindset checkpoint: Data is feedback, not failure. Every click and conversion tells you where to lean in and where to pivot.

Income goal: $600,000 cumulative revenue by end of Month 9. Premium pricing locked in, brand refreshed, book launch runway active.

Months 10-12: Build Your Dream Team and Take Your Victory Lap

You've made it this far. Clients are booked, your newsletter has traction, your book is on deck (or about to launch), and your revenue graph looks like a ski slope headed straight up. This final stretch is about converting momentum into stability, and preparing for a future where growth doesn't depend on burning yourself out.

The truth? You can't scale by doing everything alone. This is the quarter where you assemble your **Lean Dream Team** (and yes, we'll go deeper into how to do this in Part Three). Whether it's a virtual assistant to wrangle your inbox, an editor to polish your drafts, or a PR strategist to amplify your book launch, the goal is the same: create leverage so every hour you work multiplies in impact. This isn't just about business hires either. It might be time to hire a cleaning service, a laundry pickup, or even a private chef. Protecting your mental bandwidth is as strategic as any funnel you'll build.

You'll also expand your offers. Add complementary services like VIP intensives, speechwriting packages, or one-day consulting sessions. These premium, time-boxed options create high-margin wins without clogging your calendar. Continue to systematize and lean into having your lean dream team keep the engine working, even when you're not.

And don't forget the spotlight. Share the results you've created for clients (anonymized if necessary). Post those income screenshots, case studies, and transformation stories. Social proof is a growth engine, and by now, you have the receipts to run it hard.

Here's the best part: this phase is your victory lap. Maybe you're prepping for your book launch with a killer PR plan. Maybe you've booked a tour stop in Paris or signed on for a keynote that pays what your old monthly salary used to be. This is where the grind of the early months cashes out in the currency of freedom—time, money, creative sovereignty. You've built something rare: a writing business that doesn't just sustain you, but elevates you.

Keep Doing

- **Write Daily.** Client work, book marketing, or newsletter —momentum matters.

- **Newsletter Publishing.** Keep the 1-2 posts per week streak alive. Add help like an editor when needed.
- **Premium Pitching.** If you have room for new clients, keep pitching, but at rates that reflect your evolution.

New for Months 10-12

- **Hire Your Dream Team.**
  - Admin support for scheduling, invoicing, and inbox zero.
  - Editor for newsletter, manuscripts, or ghostwriting projects.
  - Bookkeeper and CPA to keep your seven-figure finances clean.
  - Strategic hires: book marketer, PR person, or ad specialist for your launch.
  - Upgrade Your Lifestyle Support: Cleaning service, laundry pickup, chef—anything that buys back time and energy.
- **Expand Your Offer Stack.** Add complementary offers like VIP days, speechwriting packages, or consulting bundles.
- **Polish and Systemize.** Automate your newsletter sequences, refine funnels, and template client workflows.
- **Maximize Your Book Launch.**
  - Finalize cover design and metadata.
  - Coordinate influencer outreach and ARC distribution.
  - Lock in preorder bonuses and ad strategy.
  - Book podcast interviews and virtual/in-person events for your launch tour.
- **Showcase Your Wins.** Share client results, testimonials, and media features. Social proof sells for you while you sleep.

Mindset checkpoint: Delegate before you think you're ready. Your highest-value work is the work only you can do.

Income goal: $1,000,000+ cumulative revenue. Book launched (or days from launch), team in place, evergreen funnels humming, brand operating like a seven-figure powerhouse.

And if you've hit this? Take a moment. Pour the champagne. You've done what most writers only dream about—you've built a business that funds your freedom, a book that amplifies your voice, and a brand that puts you in rooms where gatekeepers used to block the door. The next chapter? It's yours to write.

Monthly Rhythms To Keep Your Writing Business Growing

Building a seven-figure writing business isn't just about what you sell. It's about how you run the empire once it starts printing gold. Most writers skip this part because they'd rather be buried in client drafts or social media doom-scrolling "aesthetic desk setups." Cute, but unprofitable.

If you want freedom, stability, and a career that doesn't make you want to fake your own death in Bali, you need a system. A rhythm. Habits that keep your business solvent and your creativity spicy. Think of these as your monthly rituals: equal parts spreadsheet swagger and soul vacation.

Track your time like a detective by installing a time tracker on your computer and seeing where your hours went. Were you building a six-figure offer, or designing your fifth graphic for a social media post nobody saw? Time is the one currency you can't print more of.

This isn't just about being efficient. Creativity requires white space. If your calendar looks like a Tetris board, you're going to write like a robot. Build in time for walks, movies in the middle of the day, staring at a wall until your next Big Idea drops.

Another thing to keep you on track is to pick one big weekly move from the above checklists. Client work pays the bills, but growth work builds the empire. This big move could be outlining your book, crafting a new series for your paid newsletter, or sending that "shoot-your-shot" pitch email to a high-net-worth client. One big move per week is 52 shots at leveling up per year.

Rhythms like this matter because chaos looks charming in an indie film, but not in your writing business.

Check your numbers. Check your time. Check your soul. Make the big moves. Take the damn vacation. Because seven figures means nothing if you're too fried to enjoy it. And the version of you twelve months from now—the one sipping a cold mocktail on the beach after a sold-out book signing—will thank you for every single rhythm you locked in today.

Power Move: Make the Roadmap Yours

Here's where you separate readers from doers: write down the damn checklist. Not later, not "when I have time"—*now*. Tape it above your desk, tuck it into your journal, or make it your laptop wallpaper if you're a digital minimalist.

This chapter isn't a cute inspirational quote. It's your blueprint. As you take the lessons you've learned from this book into the real world, keep that checklist beside you like a co-pilot. Scribble notes in the margins to help you execute on what comes next. Circle the parts that excite you. Highlight the ones that scare you because those are usually the ones that move the needle.

Ask yourself:

- What does this roadmap look like for me?
- Which pieces of this puzzle do I already have, and which ones do I need to build from scratch?
- What will make these milestones feel like mine, not just someone else's plan?

And here's the kicker: pencil in your Day One. That's the day you stop underlining clever sentences and start stacking wins. Circle it in your calendar. Announce it to your accountability partner. Hell, post it on social media or your newsletter if you're feeling bold.

Because consuming information doesn't change lives. Action does. And this power move—printing the roadmap, customizing it, and committing to a start date—is how you guarantee this doesn't become another "someday" dream.

Your million-dollar year is waiting. The clock starts when you say it does.

Amy's Field Notes: Why I Hired a Business Coach (And Why Support is Key to Growth)

In the late summer of 2025, Kyle and I hopped on Zoom with our new business coach—a fellow USC grad who now works with creative entrepreneurs. If you're wondering, *Amy, why the hell do you need a business coach when you literally wrote a book about writing for money and power?* Great question. Here's the thing: success isn't static. The moves that get you to six figures are not the moves that keep you sane when you've hit seven.

We'd barely finished the first round of "How's life?" small talk when she hit me with a reality check. In fifteen minutes, my new coach dismantled assumptions I didn't even know I had: how I was running my team, what my processes looked like (or didn't) and why I was unknowingly creating my own bottlenecks.

She said something that stuck to the effect of: *You hired people to free up your time. But if they don't know what success looks like, you're not running a team. You're inviting people into your collective chaos.*

Ouch. But true.

Here's my confession: I never had formal business training. My "corporate" experience was working in the Hollywood trenches, where the org chart was basically a series of egos in descending order and where "management style" meant texting your boss at 2 a.m. to confirm whether their dog preferred sparkling or still water. I knew how to write scripts and survive messy wrap parties, but profit margins? Scalable systems? Not on the syllabus.

So when I built my writing business, I winged it. And for a while, winging it worked—until it didn't. The newsletter was growing. The client roster was stacked. And suddenly, I was drowning in emails and wondering why the hell I was still working nights if I had a team.

Cue the business coach. She introduced me to ideas I'd previously rolled my eyes at: weekly check-ins, 30-60-90 day plans, clear KPIs. I thought, *That's for tech bros in Patagonia vests, not for writers like me.* But guess what? Once I implemented them, everything clicked. My team knew what a "win" looked like. They started hitting targets without me micromanaging. And for the first time, my six-figure paid newsletter ran without me hovering—or even without me having to hit "send" on a single email.

That's true freedom. Freedom to plan a month-long trip to Asia where I'll be fully offline while the newsletter and the rest of my business hums along like a well-oiled machine.

Here's the bigger takeaway: you can cling to the I'm-a-creative-not-a-CEO identity, or you can embrace the uncomfortable truth that creative freedom requires some entrepreneurial muscle. And you don't have to grow that muscle alone. Hire help. Join masterminds like our quarterly mastermind group over at MakeWritingYour-Job.com. Find mentors who've walked the path. Because yes, you can figure everything out yourself—but why would you, when the shortcut is a Zoom call away?

If the idea of building a business feels foreign or "too corporate," remember this: you're not recreating the cubicle farm you escaped from. You're designing something different. Something built for the way you want to live. Systems are here to give creativity oxygen.

The question is: will you resist those systems out of fear, or will you adopt the ones that buy you the life you actually want?

Your call. I know mine—I'm booking my flight to Asia.

PART III

HOW TO SCALE
THE POWER PLAY

13

CREATING YOUR SAFETY NET: FINANCIAL, LEGAL, AND HEALTH SYSTEMS FOR SUSTAINABLE SUCCESS

When you're a freelancer, author, or self-employed creative, one of the hardest early lessons is that *you* are the business. You're the CEO of the page. You're the marketing department, the billing department, the customer service rep—at least at first.

It can feel exposing as hell. I remember when I was just getting started. I was drowning in work, taking on ghostwriting projects, self-publishing books, launching paid subscriptions. I would think, *What if something goes wrong? What if I make a mistake on a contract? What if I get sick?*

I felt vulnerable. Because I was.

Over time, I learned to protect myself. I got strategic about my business structure. I hired a lawyer to review my contracts. I found a CPA who could help me with the money side of things. I learned the difference between a scramble and a system.

And while I can't give you "how to do it all" in one chapter, I can share the fundamental building blocks that helped me move from exposed to protected.

Whether you're selling your books, your services, or your ideas, these are the basics that worked for me so that I could weather storms, reduce stress, and build a writing career that actually lasts.

Remember: the tips I share in this book aren't financial or legal advice. That's why you need to find those professionals to help you in those areas.

The High Cost of Burning Out

When my memoir roster exploded in 2020, I thought I was killing it. Back-to-back client calls, late-night writing marathons, triple espressos at midnight to get everything done. I celebrated the surge in invoices, until my body issued its own.

In early 2021, I had an autoimmune diagnosis that knocked me flat, which I've written about before. However, the root of my illness was in part from the cycle of burnout I had placed myself in. As it turns out, chronic stress isn't just "feeling tired." It's a full-body system crash. The World Health Organization now classifies burnout as an occupational phenomenon.[1] And the global price tag for lost productivity is estimated north of $300 billion every year.[2]

I learned about burnout from the legendary book *Burnout: The Secret to Unlocking the Stress Cycle* by Emily and Amelia Nagoski, which I recommend reading if you've ever waved off stress as a harmless factor in your life. Some of the strategies in their book are foundational to health: using exercise as a remedy to a stressful event so you can close the loop on a stress cycle, and making it your personal mission to find ways to reduce stress in your life.

If you're thinking about building a six- or seven-figure writing career, you need to understand this: there is no empire if the emperor lies dead on the floor.

---

1. World Health Organization, "Burn-out an Occupational Phenomenon: International Classification of Diseases," *WHO.int*, accessed 2025, https://www.who.int/news/item/28-05-2019-burn-out-an-occupational-phenomenon-international-classification-of-diseases

2. *Runn*, "Burnout Statistics: 28+ Scary Stats and Facts," *Runn Blog*, accessed 2025, https://www.runn.io/blog/burnout-statistics

Don't treat your body like an unlimited resource. Build systems that protect your energy, your time, and your health the way you'd protect your bank account or intellectual property.

Because the cost of ignoring burnout isn't just personal misery—it's lost creative momentum, stalled income, and long-term health damage that can drain your savings in months.

Fortify Your Financial Moat

If money is the fuel for your writing business, you need to make sure your tank doesn't have holes. Financial resiliency is about being able to say no to bad clients, cover emergencies without panic, and invest in your growth.

Here are the basics all writers can put into place with the help of their accountant:

- **Emergency Fund.** Six to twelve months of living costs parked in a high-yield savings account.
- **Profit Buckets.** Some writers find it helpful to have separate accounts for taxes, operating costs, and personal pay.
- **Barbell Income.** Anchor one predictable retainer (like luxury ghostwriting) and one scalable line (like books or courses). This is why we talk about both passive income (book royalties) semi-active income (subscriptions for paid newsletters) and active income (freelance ghostwriting) in this book: having a variety of income streams can help you reduce risk.

This isn't necessarily fun or flashy advice. It's "boring" on purpose. Because the goal isn't to flex. The goal is to stay calm when your car breaks down, your dog needs surgery, or you get handed an unexpected medical bill.

This buffer is what allows you to take creative risks, because you know you can land safely if you fall.

As always, talk to your CPA to build the right strategies for you.

Suit Up with Legal Armor

When I was getting started, the idea of "legal stuff" made me want to crawl under my desk. But ignoring it doesn't make the risk go away.

If you're selling anything—books, subscriptions, services—you're running a business. And businesses need armor.

Talk to your lawyer about what might work for you and your writing business, bringing up topics like...

- **LLC or S-Corp.** Shields personal assets from business lawsuits. Choose what fits your situation with the help of your CPA and lawyer.
- **Ironclad Contracts.** Get a lawyer to draft one solid master agreement you can adapt forever. Include things like kill fees, revision limits, and go into detail with your lawyer about what will help protect your unique offer and workflow the best.
- **IP Protection.** Talk to your lawyer about how to register copyrights, trademark your imprint, and discuss other ways to protect your intellectual property.
- **Errors and Omissions Insurance.** Your CPA and lawyer may be able to recommend the right type of insurance for your business. This type is sometimes included in general liability insurance, and covers defamation or copyright claims for ghostwriters and indie publishers.

Yes, you'll pay some money up front to talk to a lawyer. But a one-hour legal consult today is cheaper than a five-figure lawsuit tomorrow.

Build this well once, and it pays you back in dividends of peace of mind and great sleep.

Health Systems That Actually Work

Forget bragging about hustle. Your health is the infrastructure that lets you do this work for decades. No one pays you to be sick, and no insurance plan can buy you back time lost to burnout.

Here's what I've built into my daily and weekly routines:

- **Movement.** 7,000-10,000 steps a day plus three weekly strength workouts, with the occasional dance or Pilates class thrown in. These workouts complete the stress cycle and keep energy levels steady.
- **Fuel.** 80% whole-food meals, low sugar, moderate caffeine. Stable blood sugar equals stable mood and focus.
- **Sleep.** 7-9 hours in a dark, screen-free bedroom. Memory consolidation, hormone balance, and anti-burnout insurance.
- **Nervous System Care.** Breathwork, meditation, or even a 15-minute walk after calls. Lowers cortisol spikes and keeps me grounded.
- **Mental Hygiene.** Therapist, mastermind group, or journaling ritual to off-load client or life stress before it festers.

These habits cost less than one emergency room visit and return compound interest in sustained creativity.

If you want to be a writer who makes six or seven figures over decades, this is non-negotiable.

Mindset: Prepare for Storms, Expect Sun

It's easy to get paralyzed by catastrophic thinking. What if the economy tanks? What if a client doesn't pay me? What if my health fails? Here's the thing: bad things will happen. The goal isn't to avoid every storm. It's to build a boat that can handle it. You buffer your money, armor your business, protect your health, and then you assume you'll figure out whatever lands on your desk. Because the truth is, *you* are the asset. If you fall apart, the whole business does. Treat yourself like the million-dollar machine you're tuning to run.

And here's where a lot of new writers wobble: when you step away from a steady paycheck into freelancing or authorship, it's easy to feel exposed. Like you've traded a steel bunker for a paper umbrella in a hurricane.

I talk to writers every day in our community at MakeWritingYour-Job.com, and I've seen it all: some quit their jobs and replace their income in three months. Others creep forward slowly, wondering if they made a mistake. Some are thriving, others are terrified, and often it's not about talent. It's about mindset. Because mindset is the rudder that keeps you moving when fear starts screaming "turn back."

Every business book on the planet preaches "avoid catastrophic risk," but here's the twist: you're not running a Fortune 500 tanker. You're a solo vessel, maybe with a lean dream team down the line, and that means your greatest vulnerability isn't the market—it's your brain. Catastrophic thinking will try to convince you that a late invoice means the end of your career or a slow month means you should go crawling back to your old boss. That spiral is how writers go broke. Not because the work dried up, but because the courage did. After all, how much do you think about the AP bio test you failed in high school? Or how embarrassing it was to get turned down by your crush in 9th grade? Time gives perspective on how big certain things feel, and worry is simply misplaced imagination. Don't kneecap your bravery with existential anxiety.

So yes, prepare for storms. Build buffers. Six to twelve months of cash buys you clarity. Smart contracts with kill fees and scope clauses act like armor plates. Sleep, hydration, and a stress outlet keep your engine from overheating. But after you've stocked your life raft? Expect sun. You cannot build an extraordinary career while staring at the horizon like it owes you a hurricane. This game demands an odd cocktail: realism to know rough seas will come, and a dash of delusion to believe your island of success is inevitable. That blend of clear-eyed prep and stubborn optimism is the mindset that separates the writers who hit six and seven figures from the ones who ghost their own dreams.

Because betting on yourself isn't just a risk. It's the only gamble where you keep the upside. Yes, you eat the uncertainty, but you also eat the reward. Every extra zero on the invoice, every new revenue stream, every reader who presses "buy" without a gatekeeper in sight —that's yours. And when the sun breaks after the storm, you'll know the truth: you didn't just survive. You built a damn good boat.

Power Move: Your Safety Net Checklist

Before you chase the big numbers, pause and ask: *What would make me feel steady and secure in this business?* For some writers, it's an emergency fund. For others, it's airtight contracts, health systems, or a circle of trusted advisors. Whatever it is for you, start identifying it now, before storms hit.

Use this checklist as a template, not gospel. Your circumstances are unique, so run these ideas past your lawyer and CPA before you act. Add what makes sense, cut what doesn't, and think creatively about what else belongs on your list so that burnout, chaos, or a single client crisis never has the power to break your business.

Here are some things to consider adding to your safety net checklist:

- Six-month emergency fund in high-yield savings
- LLC or S-Corp formation with lawyer-vetted client contracts
- Errors and Omissions insurance active
- Weekly movement and recovery schedule on your calendar
- Quarterly financial and legal reviews booked
- Daily stress-cycle completion ritual logged
- Support network (coach, therapist, community, mastermind group) engaged

Check these boxes and the next market crash, lawsuit threat, or midnight cortisol spike becomes a pothole—not a cliff.

Building your safety net doesn't make you paranoid. It makes you prepared.

Amy's Field Notes: How Burnout Taught Me Resiliency

As I've shared a few times in this book already, I was diagnosed with an autoimmune condition in 2021. At that point, I'd pushed myself too far, ignoring every warning sign. All-nighters, skipped meals, endless Zoom calls, constant client demands.

The diagnosis felt like betrayal. I was in my late twenties. I thought I was "healthy."

What I didn't realize was how many small, bad habits had compounded into a health crisis. And the financial cost? Brutal.

I burned through savings on alternative therapies, personal trainers, nutritionists, experimental treatments. Even with good income, it was destabilizing. My insurance didn't cover much of it. I felt vulnerable in a way I hadn't since I first started freelancing.

But here's what I learned: having that safety net was what let me survive it. Without savings, I couldn't have hired help. I couldn't have paid for the meds, the copays, the specialists.

I had to rethink everything about my business. I raised my rates. I cut hours. I got strategic about what work I took on. I built better systems.

Most importantly, I started thinking about resilience on every level:

- **Emotional Resilience** so I could handle crises without falling apart.
- **Financial Resilience** so unexpected bills wouldn't put me underwater.
- **Physical Resilience** so my body wouldn't revolt again.

That resiliency is why I can say no to bad-fit projects. Why I can take days off without guilt. Why I show up more powerfully for the clients I do choose to work with.

If you're not resilient in one or more of those areas, that's your work right now. Because you can't build anything sustainable if you're fried, broke, or broken.

Resiliency is what gives you the freedom to be bold. To write what you want. To live how you want.

Build it now. You'll never regret it.

14

BUILD YOUR LEAN DREAM
TEAM: SCALING WITHOUT
LOSING YOUR FREEDOM

When writers ask me about scaling their business, they often imagine this big, complicated empire. Maybe they've seen those posts: "I scaled to seven figures with an agency model!" What they don't see is the loss of profit margins, or the increased headaches.

Scaling as a writer doesn't mean hiring a dozen people and playing middle manager for the rest of your life. Scaling, when done right, is about buying back your most valuable resource: your time. It's about protecting your energy, focusing on the work you love most, and making sure you're not the bottleneck for every single task.

I've tried different models. I experimented with agency-style offerings. I've run courses. Personally? Didn't love them. What works for me is partnership. Instead of bringing everything in-house, I refer my clients out to trusted collaborators—book designers, marketers, editors. I don't have to manage their work. I don't pay their payroll. They're experts in their own businesses, and my clients get better results because of it.

That's what this chapter is about: not building a giant company that owns you, but building a lean, effective network of freelance specialists you can call on when needed. It's how you keep creative control while getting out of your own way.

The Lone-Wolf Lie

Early in my career I wore isolation like a badge of honor. I wrote every word, formatted every invoice, redesigned my website at 2 a.m. after completing a copywriting assignment. I thought hustle and "I can do it all myself!" equaled success.

The reality? Bottlenecks, blown launch dates, creative fatigue masquerading as "work ethic."

Writing can be solitary. But running a writing *business* should not be. My business only leveled up when I started hiring true specialists.

When I hired a brand photographer, my site actually looked like a professional service instead of a high school project. When I hired a website designer, the clunky DIY site transformed into a real sales tool. When I hired expert cover designers, my books looked like they deserved to be on shelves.

Each of these investments let me focus on what I do best—writing—while elevating the way clients and readers perceived my work.

If you want to scale without burning out, you have to let go of the lone-wolf fantasy.

Why Small, Specialist Teams Beat Big Staffs

It's tempting to think that growing your business means hiring a big team, but I think you need to resist this impulse to keep control over your work life. Small teams stay nimble. Fewer people mean clearer communication, faster execution, and less overhead.

Harvard data scientists Dashun Wang and James Evans analyzed millions of papers and patents and found that compact teams spark more disruptive breakthroughs than sprawling groups. The sweet spot: five or fewer contributors.[1] Lean pods move faster, coordinate intuitively, and keep incentives crystal-clear, which is exactly what a writer-run empire needs.

Freelancers, contractors, and partners let you grow your impact without bloating your expenses. You hire only for what you need, when you need it.

Instead of a generalist trying to do everything, you get top-tier specialists in the exact slice of work you want to outsource.

Big companies are overrated, especially now. The future is freelance.

Enter the Lean Dream Team Concept for Writers and Creator CEOs

Think of your dream team like an elite heist crew: every person is the best at their specific role.

Your goal isn't to build a massive organization. It's to assemble a roster of people who can help you deliver exceptional results without adding bureaucracy.

Focus on specialists: people who do one thing incredibly well. A book marketer who can help you nail the layout of your book's launch page. An editor who's laser-focused on your genre. A publicist who focuses on book launches.

And use technology instead of people where you can. Avoid hiring project managers or assistants for tasks that a good workflow tool can handle.

Sometimes, the role you need to hire for is to help you on a personal level, not a business one. Maybe you're spending hours every week doing laundry at a broken laundromat. Outsource that to a pickup service so you can reclaim that time for writing, or rest. (Because rest is an important part of your process, too!)

---

1. L. Fiona Wu, Dashun Wang, and James A. Evans, "Research: When Small Teams Are Better Than Big Ones," *Harvard Business Review*, accessed 2025, https://hbr.org/2019/02/research-when-small-teams-are-better-than-big-ones

Here's how I recommend approaching the hiring process:

1. **Start with the bottleneck.** The single point of failure that is slowing you down the most. If you could wave a magic wand and solve a problem, who would appear to help you?

2. **Pay by the deliverable, not the hour.** Build trust with a flat-rate project first. Later, if you know them well, hourly might make sense, but consider setting an hourly cap or budget so it doesn't balloon.

3. **Document once, delegate forever.** Any time you hire for a repeatable task, have the freelancer document the workflow so you're not reinventing the wheel next time.

4. **Retain decision control.** You make the final calls. Collaboration is good. Committees are bad. Don't hire people who need constant hand-holding.

When I first tried to hire help, I thought I needed a virtual assistant, but it was too early for that. I didn't need someone to manage my inbox in the beginning stages of my growth. I needed real specialists and people who could do things I couldn't. The right hire isn't just someone who helps, although that can be valuable later. But when you're just starting to accelerate, you need laser-focused professionals who can solve high-value problems.

Note what's missing here: middle managers, account coordinators, project managers who need constant oversight. Every dollar you spend should go toward expertise—not layers of communication or permission-seeking.

Avoiding the Big-Agency Trap

I once hired a storied PR firm. Five-figure retainer. Weekly Zooms. Fancy strategy decks. The result? Fewer media hits than the solo publicist I hired later for a fraction of the cost.

Agencies chase margin. Specialists chase mastery.

When you work with an agency, you're often paying for their office rent, their overhead, their assistant's salary—not necessarily better work.

That's why I'm all about hiring specialists, not outsourcing to one giant, expensive, generalist company.

You want to pay for outcomes, not bureaucracy.

Types of Freelancers and Services You Can Hire to Make Your Life Easier

If you want to work smarter—not just harder—it helps to know exactly who you can bring on board to lighten the load. Below is an expanded guide to the types of specialists, freelancers, and service providers you might consider.

The goal isn't to hire all of them. It's to see where your energy and time are leaking away, then match the right help to the right problem.

Here are some freelance hires you may want to consider making as your writing business grows:

- **Editor or Proofreader.** Catches typos and small errors you're blind to after reading your own work a dozen times. This doesn't just prevent embarrassment—it protects your reputation for quality, saving time on back-and-forth with clients or readers who spot mistakes. You could also hire a developmental editor to help with feedback on the content level of a book, blog post, or newsletter.
- **Book Designer or Cover Designer.** Creates a professional, market-ready package that signals quality at first glance. They help your book stand out in crowded marketplaces and improve reader trust before they even turn a page.
- **Brand Photographer.** Elevates your online presence with polished, consistent images that make you look like the pro you are. Quality visuals build authority and help you command higher rates.

- **Website Designer.** Turns a DIY, clunky site into a frictionless sales tool. A great website not only looks good but makes it easier for readers or clients to buy, book, or sign up.
- **Graphic Designer.** Brings your ideas to life visually—from social media graphics to sales pages to pitch decks. Professional design sets you apart from generic templates and reinforces your brand.
- **Video Editor.** Transforms raw footage into polished marketing content, online courses, or longform videos that can drive traffic, sales, or subscriptions. Saves you hours wrestling with software and ensures a professional result.
- **Book Publicist.** Handles outreach to media, podcasts, and reviewers to get your book seen. They navigate the world of publicity so you don't have to spend weeks cold-emailing people who never reply.
- **Book Marketing Strategist.** Develops a customized plan to actually sell your book, from pricing to ads to launch strategy. Prevents you from publishing into the void and can help you get real results.
- **Paid Ads Manager.** Plans and runs ad campaigns on search engines, social media, and book publishing platforms. Instead of guessing (and wasting money), you get targeted, trackable campaigns designed to pay for themselves.

Personal-Side Helpers

Outsourcing isn't just for your business. Buying back time and peace of mind in your personal life can be just as valuable—sometimes more so.

Here are some potential hires for your personal life:

- **House Cleaner.** Gives you back hours each week and the

mental relief of a tidy, welcoming space. Reduces decision fatigue about "when will I finally mop the floor?"

- **Laundry Service.** Turns a multi-hour chore into five minutes of drop-off and pick-up. No more waiting at broken machines or folding for days.
- **Personal Chef or Meal Delivery Service.** Ensures you eat nourishing, tasty meals without shopping, cooking, or cleaning. Supports health goals while freeing you for focused work or rest.
- **Grocery Delivery.** Eliminates crowded aisles, checkout lines, and impulse buys. Saves time and mental energy for more important decisions.
- **Babysitter or Nanny.** Gives parents protected work time or restorative breaks—an investment in both income and sanity.
- **Personal Trainer.** Customizes workouts to your goals while keeping you accountable. Supports the physical resilience you need for a demanding creative career.
- **Nutritionist.** Helps you fine-tune eating habits to support focus, energy, and long-term health. Especially valuable if health issues have ever threatened your productivity.
- **Therapist or Coach.** Offers structured space to process stress, set goals, and develop better habits. Reduces the emotional load you carry alone, making you more effective in business and life.

The bottom line? Hiring help isn't just about saving time. It's about protecting your focus for the work that matters most, reducing stress that leads to burnout, and improving the quality of everything you ship.

Often the difference between a struggling freelancer and a thriving business owner isn't who works harder, it's who knows when to delegate.

Power Move: The Outsourcing Audit

Grab a notebook or open a spreadsheet, because this move starts with clarity. Begin by listing the tasks that eat up most of your time each week. Identify every repetitive chore, every admin loop, every creative bottleneck. For each one, jot down how many hours it takes, whether you enjoy it or dread it, and whether it truly demands your unique expertise. Be honest: does sending invoices or editing captions really require your genius? Probably not.

Next, calculate your average hourly rate based on your business income. Once you know what an hour of your time is worth, compare it to what it would cost to delegate. Any task you could pay someone less than your hourly rate to handle is a prime candidate for outsourcing. Highlight the top one or two items you can let go of immediately. These are the tasks that, if done by someone else, free up the most time or mental energy for high-value work, or simply give you space to breathe.

Remember, scaling is about buying back time so you can build smarter, not heavier. The real flex is creating a business where your brain does the work only your brain can do.

Amy's Field Notes: Time for Value

A few years ago, I was reading Shonda Rhimes' *Year of Yes*, and one sentiment really stuck with me. She wrote about how people constantly asked her, "How do you do it all?" And she answered honestly: "I don't. I have a lot of help."

That line hit me hard. Because it's easy to look at successful people—writers with bestsellers, entrepreneurs running multiple projects—and imagine they've got some secret superpower for squeezing 36 hours into our 24. But the truth is, most of them aren't doing it all themselves. They've just gotten really good at buying back their time.

That lesson shows up in nearly every business book I've read since. Don't just work *in* the business, work *on* it. Build systems that can run without you hovering over every detail. Make sure your operation still functions even if you step away, get sick, or log in from the other side of the world.

And I know what you might be thinking, especially if you're a writer. *But my thinking is the business. My words are the product.*

True. But I hope by now, reading this book, you see there's so much more to the engine that makes a writing career sustainable. There's your newsletter audience. Your royalties from past books. Your freelance clients who pay big invoices and keep you going. There are all these revenue streams that keep delivering even when you're not at the keyboard 24/7. You can absolutely scale beyond the number of hours you personally work in a week.

A while back, Kyle and I sat down and did an audit of our time. Both of us run our own businesses, and after we stopped being full-time digital nomads and settled down in San Francisco, we realized we felt perpetually "time poor." We kept asking ourselves, how are we always busy yet always behind?

So we wrote it all out. Every recurring task, every time-suck, every errand. And the results surprised us.

For example, Kyle was spending hours each week wrestling with the laundry situation. Our beautiful old home has plenty of charm, but also some serious inconveniences—namely, the ground-floor laundry machines that never work. We'd end up hauling loads to a busy laundromat blocks away, often having to wait around and losing chunks of prime work time.

At first, paying for a laundry service felt ridiculous. We'd always done it ourselves. Why would we spend money on something so "basic"?

But when we ran the math, it was obvious. The cost of the service was far less than the value of the hours we'd get back. Those would be hours we could use to work, rest, or actually enjoy our lives.

Same thing happened with meals. While writing this book, I've been spending hours a day deep in the material, which is both joyful and demanding work. Meanwhile, Kyle and I still had to figure out dinner every night. We were too wiped to cook from scratch, kept defaulting to eating out, and realized it wasn't sustainable.

We finally signed up for a local meal delivery service that specializes in plant-based, whole-food meals. Each week, our fridge gets stocked with fresh, healthy options. Now we don't have to think about what's for dinner or waste time cooking when our brains are fried.

I read a quote recently that stuck with me. It said something along the lines of: imagine reading a beautiful book that moves you deeply, but every time you turn a page, you can never turn back.

That's life. Every day you live is a page you can't reread. You can remember it, but you can't relive it.

That's why your time is precious.

So take this chapter seriously. Do the audit. Make the list. Figure out what drains you, what you can let go of, what you can pay someone else to handle so you can focus on the writing only you can do.

Because buying back your time isn't just a business strategy. It's a life strategy.

Your time is precious. Treat it as such.

15

HUMANS VS. AI: WIN WITH TASTE

If you've made it this far, I'm going to assume you've found at least something in this book worth your time. Maybe you're already on the road to building your own six- or seven-figure writing empire. If so, that's awesome. I'm genuinely happy for you. Because what you're doing is cool. It's bold. And it's rare.

But since you've stuck with me this long, I want to share something that might surprise you. This book you're reading right now? I wrote it with the help of AI—in less than a month of focused deep work. 83 hours to be exact, and that includes rewrites! For comparison, my last nonfiction book, *Six-Figure Freelance Writer*, took an entire year of dedicated work to write. I'd estimate that book took me closer to 300 hours to complete.

I know that some of you just flinched at the admission of using AI to write this book. Maybe you're annoyed. Maybe you're flat-out mad. I get it. A lot of writers see AI as something to fear. I understand that because I felt the same way at first. When these tools first started showing up, I dismissed them immediately. I even wrote a whole newsletter essay making fun of them when these tools first came out —pointing out all their dumb mistakes and saying "look how bad this is. These tech bros think they can replace us? Idiots."

After all, writing is about meaning. About insight. About the human spirit. As technologist Paul Graham put it: *good writing is good thinking*. Technology can't imitate those things, so why should I care?

But as I've been experimenting over the last few years, I changed my mind. I learned these AI tools can be incredible amplifiers of our work. They're not replacements. They're accelerators. And honestly, I think every serious writer who wants to stay competitive is going to use them in some way. The next generation of writers will understand AI, how it works, and what it's good (and terrible) at.

Every major shift in technology has changed creative work. The printing press changed who could write books. The typewriter changed how fast we could produce them. Computers made editing a thousand times easier. And now, AI tools are here.

The mistake here is believing writers are just typists. That if your fingers aren't hammering every word, it "doesn't count." Writers aren't typists. Writers are thinkers. Philosophers. Storytellers. Communicators. Whether your words end up in a novel, a screenplay, an ad, a podcast script, or a newsletter doesn't matter—the thinking behind them is your real value.

So if you have access to a tool that can help you type faster, organize your thoughts better, or give you more time to think deeply— why *wouldn't* you use it?

This chapter is my attempt to share how I think about AI, not as an enemy, but as a tool. I want you to see how to use it without losing your voice, your craft, or your edge.

Because at the end of the day, this is about using technology to keep your work sharp. It's about keeping you competitive in a world that's changing fast. And it's about remembering that time is your most valuable resource.

The Latest Boogey-Man in a Long Parade

When the typewriter muscled onto desks, purists mourned the death of penmanship. Radios were supposed to kill books, computer animation was supposed to replace artists and actors, blogging was the graveyard of literature until social media became the new tombstone. Generative AI is simply the next specter.

Fear is understandable. A November 2024 study from the University of Pittsburgh found that, in blind tests, readers preferred AI-generated poems to those by Shakespeare, Plath, and Eliot.[1] Headlines screamed *"Robots Out-Write Humans!"* and poets braced for pink slips.

But here's the thing, this cycle is as old as technology itself. When telephones were invented, there were rumors about phantoms in the phone lines. People don't really fear technology itself. They fear change.

That fear is natural. Change is relentless, and it always reshapes the way we work. We don't have an abundance of stable hands or lamplighters anymore. Instead, we have social media managers, influencers, bloggers, coaches—jobs no Renaissance philosopher could have imagined. The shape of work evolves. Some roles disappear, new ones emerge. That's always been true.

Change is everywhere. It can be unsettling. I understand that fear deeply. But the antidote to fear is knowledge. Knowledge is the flashlight you carry into the dark. If you're feeling anxious about AI, don't turn away. Learn more about how it works. Then make your own call about how you want to integrate it into your life and your work.

Tools Evolve, Perspective Endures

On my 31st birthday, Kyle booked a private tour of San Francisco's Arion Press, the last U.S. book factory that casts metal type, letterpress-prints sheets, and creates hand-bound volumes under one roof. Each edition costs roughly $2,000 to buy and months to create. Why does an old-fashioned foundry thrive in an e-book world? Because connoisseurs pay for the inscription of care and for fine art

---

1. Jan Oschinski and Natalia Melnychuk, "Large Language Models as Job Search Engines: The Case of ChatGPT," *Scientific Reports* 14, no. 1 (2024), accessed 2025, https://www.nature.com/articles/s41598-024-76900-1

they can feel in the grain of cotton paper and the glint of a hand-set comma.

AI will flood the market with serviceable prose the way mass-market paperbacks once flooded corner drugstores. Arion Press survives this flood by swimming upstream, not by scooping buckets. Writers can do the same. Let algorithms handle the deluge while you craft the limited-edition narrative only you can sign.

Practical Ways to Put Robots on Payroll

If you're going to use AI tools, the real power is knowing what they're actually good at, and where they fall apart without you. I don't see AI as a replacement for human creativity and thoughtfulness. I see it as hiring the world's cheapest, fastest, always-available intern.

Used well, AI can take over tedious grunt work and free up your brain for the thinking, judgment, and voice only you can bring.

Here are a few of the ways I've seen AI shine for writers:

- **Transcript Summarizing.** AI can process long interviews or recordings and produce concise summaries or even structured notes. Instead of re-listening for hours, you get time back to hunt for sharper angles or deeper anecdotes.
- **Outline Expansion.** If you feed AI a rough skeleton of your argument or chapter, it can help flesh out subpoints you might have missed. Then it's on you to inject contrarian takes, real-world details, or unexpected metaphors—the stuff that makes writing yours.
- **Ideation and Brainstorming.** Stuck for headline variations? Blog topics? Chapter titles? AI can spit out dozens in seconds. You might toss most of them, but one can spark the perfect angle you wouldn't have found on your own.
- **Research Assistance.** AI is surprisingly good at unearthing links, suggesting sources, or helping you track down that quote you half-remember but can't find. It's like

having a junior researcher who knows where to look, which can save you the search engine rabbit hole.

- **Fact Aggregation.** Need a list of laws in all 50 states? Major events in a year? AI can assemble the bones fast, but your job is to apply judgment: which fact matters, which detail changes the reader's decision? Certain AI tools are better than others at research (look for the ones with lower hallucination rates) so pick the model that best suits your needs.
- **Advanced Proofreading.** While it can't replace a professional editor, AI is good at catching repeated words, confusing phrasing, or mechanical errors that slip through human fatigue. Think of it as one extra pair of tireless eyes.
- **Copy Drafting and Polishing.** Stuck writing cold outreach, proposals, or marketing blurbs? AI can provide starting points. Your job is to add authentic voice and cut the generic filler.

Used this way, AI isn't your ghostwriter. It's your unpaid, 24/7 research assistant, idea iterator, and typo catcher. If you treat AI like a junior on your team, you'll keep control of your voice while buying back the time and energy to do what really matters: thinking clearly and writing powerfully.

Taste: The Competitive Moat

Good taste is cultivated through inputs: reading widely, traveling, watching obscure documentaries, talking to octogenarian jazz musicians. Garbage in, garbage out applies to humans and machines alike, but you alone decide which obsessions to feed the algorithm that is your mind.

A prompt cannot supply worldview, heartbreak, or the goosebumps you felt hearing your favorite band live. Only a writer can.

If the Robots Ever Wake Up…

Should AI attain self-directed consciousness, your freelance writing rates will be the least of humanity's worries. Instead, maybe learn how to operate a laser gun or whatever tool at your disposal in the robot wars.

Until then, remember: the tools can imitate structure, but they cannot mint soul. Your signature perspective is still the rarest commodity on the internet.

Power Move: Your AI Deep Dive

It's time for you to take your own deep dive into AI. If you haven't started yet, this is your nudge. Because ignoring these tools won't stop them from evolving. But learning how they work gives you options, leverage, and a competitive edge.

While you're exploring those resources, take the time to do your own audit. Identify the writing tasks, business chores, or research steps that you could potentially outsource to AI. Consider where these tools can buy back your time so you can reinvest it into the thinking, strategizing, and crafting only you can do.

Amy's Field Notes: Owning Change, Owning Your Career

This past year, I went out to dinner in San Francisco with Kyle and a mutual friend who's a Hollywood writer. We were catching up, eating incredible naan and tikka masala at a great Indian restaurant in the Mission, talking about work and how Hollywood feels like it's on fire right now.

But our friend? He was doing the things I've been talking about in this book. Building his freelancing career. Funding his own film projects. Finding ways to transcend the gatekeepers. Taking ownership of his path instead of waiting for permission.

During dinner, I brought up AI. Not to preach, but because I was genuinely curious about his thoughts. I know that for a lot of people in Hollywood, AI is practically a curse word. I get why. There's fear that the studios and gatekeepers will use it against them. There's frustration that so many AI models were trained on artists' work without any real credit or payment.

I was half-expecting my friend to bristle. But instead, he surprised me. He was pretty positive about it. Open to it. We talked about how, yes, there's risk—but also opportunity. How the only real way to get power over these tools is to understand them, to learn what they can and can't do, to use them intentionally instead of ignoring them.

And it's not just him. I'm hearing that shift in a lot of the writing community these days. More and more people quietly admit they're using AI to brainstorm, organize, accelerate their workflow, even if they'd never admit it on social media.

I'll be honest with you. I was nervous about admitting that I used AI as a tool during the writing of this book. I wondered: *Am I going to get backlash? Am I going to see readers trashing it, denouncing me for daring to use these tools?* I see that energy online all the time. I see people burning books they discover were touched by AI, canceling creators who admit they use it.

I understand that rage. Truly. Because before I built my writing business, I felt exploited by the gatekeepers too. I know what it's like to feel like the only way to have power is to reject the machine entirely. And AI gets lumped in with these huge institutions and gatekeepers, when in reality it has the potential to give you a lot of freedom over your own career.

What I've realized is that real power as a writer comes from understanding the tools on the table and choosing what you want to use.

That's why I'm being transparent with you. That's why I'm sharing my thoughts on AI here and why I'll keep sharing more as part of the content I put out on my newsletters.

That doesn't mean everyone has to use AI. Just like some writers still swear by handwriting drafts or typewriters, just like some book lovers prize letterpress editions made one at a time by hand—there will always be space for different processes, for different philosophies of making art.

But here's what's true: AI is here to stay. And if you refuse to use it to handle grunt work or streamline your process, you may find yourself falling behind. I don't say that to scare you. I say it because I've seen firsthand what these tools can do.

These tools have helped me take the chaotic ideas in my head and get them onto the page fast enough to finish this book on a schedule that would have been impossible otherwise.

And maybe you'll read this and think, *Well, I don't like this book.* That's fine. I hope you find a book that's perfect for you. Because my goal isn't for you to love my book at any cost, it's for you to have the writing career you want.

That's why I'm sharing all of this with you, even if it risks backlash. Because I want you to feel like your writing career is in your own hands. That you're the one at the helm. That you can greenlight your own work.

That's why I wrote this book. So you can say yes to yourself. So you can have the knowledge, the systems, and the mindset to build the writing life you actually want.

I hope you find this transparency valuable. And above all, I hope you use it to help your readers, to tell the stories only you can tell, to change the world in your own way.

Tools come and go, but the legacy that us writers leave behind lasts forever.

16

TRAVELING THE WORLD WITH YOUR WRITING BUSINESS AND CREATIVE RETREATS

Picture this: dawn in Singapore, and the streets shimmer like they've been rinsed in gold. Ivy drapes over colonial facades in Chinatown, and somewhere behind me, a coffee grinder hums like a slow jazz riff. I'm sipping a $9 pour-over at a hip coffeeshop, the kind of cup that feels like a small sacrament, when my day begins.

Then I slide into a crisp, air-conditioned car. By noon I'm seated across from my client who has trusted me with her life story, a woman who practically owns the corner table at a sleek lunch bar inside an upscale mall in Singapore. The place feels like California wrapped in glass and green—think Los Angeles, but with better architecture and heftier air-conditioning. We talk about her book, its next act, and by the time my salad is gone we're mapping her future like two co-conspirators planning a heist.

Later, Kyle and I duck into indoor gardens hosting massive greenhouses and waterfalls. Hours blur. We end up 57 floors up at the rooftop bar Ce La Vi, mocktails sweating in their crystal glasses, watching the Singapore skyline blush as the sun folds itself into the bay. The view looks stolen from a billionaire's screensaver. I spent that sunset savoring the life I had created for myself, and taking in a city unlike I'd ever seen before.

What follows in this chapter is a framework for designing your life like a passport-stamped collage while keeping the revenue engine humming. Because when borders blur and remote work erases time zones, the old map of "work here, vacation there" is obsolete. You can take your book draft to Barcelona. Your client flies you out to meet in Greece. Your life and your prose will be richer for it.

As with every chapter in this book, I encourage you to put your dreams and ideal life first. If you don't want to be traveling every few months, then design a different idea of what writing and travel looks like for you. Maybe you're craving a staycation and a massage somewhere near your home over a European vacation. But if your fingers itch to book an overseas flight and maybe an adventure that leaves you lost in a creative wonderland in a foreign country? Read on.

From Mini-Retirements to Creative Power Plays

I read *The 4-Hour Workweek* by Tim Ferriss at a formative moment in my life. It was the kind of season where everything feels possible if you just crack the right code. Tim Ferriss wasn't pitching passive income as a beach fantasy. He was asking a bigger question: *What if the life you crave didn't have to wait for retirement? What if you could carve out sabbaticals in the middle of your working years and have a string of extended interludes where you learn, explore, and live like a human instead of a hamster?*

He called them "mini-retirements." And two decades later, his idea still holds. In fact, it's even easier to execute now more than ever. Swap the drop-shipping store for a paid newsletter and you've got a lean, automated revenue stream that can bankroll your own four-hour workweek. I know because I've done it. With my newsletter humming on subscription autopilot, I can disappear for a week or a month without watching my income flatline.

Ferriss was the original digital nomad before social media turned the term into a thirst trap. He championed remote work when it was a punchline at corporate happy hours. These days, the remote work infrastructure is undeniable and nomads flourish, typing away at cafes and coworking spaces all over the world.

But here's where I diverge from Ferriss: I don't believe in building a life you need to escape from. If your dream scenario still makes you itch for an exit, something's broken in the design. Instead of plotting a "break" from work, I'm interested in weaving creativity and autonomy so tightly into the fabric of your days that every workday feels like a soft launch of freedom.

That said, deliberate retreats matter. Your ideas deserve oxygen. My version of a mini-retirement? A creative sabbatical. Think one to four weeks of space engineered for input, not output. Earlier this year I spent ten days in the Tuscan countryside with a bestselling author and a circle of incredible female writers, which I shared with you earlier in this book. We wrote. We workshopped. We talked until midnight under string lights while wine glasses warmed in the evening heat. I came home with a notebook stuffed with ideas and a nervous system that felt like it had been rebooted at the factory.

That's the power move. Create room for serendipity without burning down your revenue engine. A retreat can look like a month in Lisbon or a weekend in Big Sur. The price tag isn't the point. The point is to live the life you want. No looming sense that your absence will collapse the empire. That's what true power buys: the power to vanish without penalty, knowing your systems are spinning cash in the background.

Bring a blank notebook. Leave your output agenda at home. Let curiosity take the wheel for a while. That white space is where your next big idea or your next six-figure client strategy tends to land. And yes, if your accountant is cool, the trip might even file under "professional development" and be a business write-off (as always, check with your CPA!). But the real ROI? A mind that feels like a clean slate and a business that hums even when you're offline.

Because here's the truth: wealth isn't just the commas in your bank account. It's owning the time to step outside your own gravity and come back sharper. That's not indulgence. That's power.

The Shadow Side of Freedom: When Power Turns Feral

Every paradise has a snake, and the Garden of Geographic Freedom is crawling with them.

On social media, digital nomads look like modern explorers. Laptops balanced on beach chairs, a mojito perched in the corner of the frame, and a constant stream of posts in gorgeous new locations. But here's the truth nobody filters: for every nomad channeling Magellan, there's another circling the drain like a drunk runaway. And sometimes those two people live in the same body, alternating shifts.

Too much freedom can feel like jet fuel—until you realize you're on fire.

Five years of living out of a suitcase taught me this: untethered living can liberate you, or it can dismantle you in slow motion. For every writer I met in Argentina who was quietly building a six-figure SEO empire between hikes to hidden waterfalls, there was another who hadn't opened their laptop in weeks because Buenos Aires nightlife runs 'til dawn and empanadas taste like temptation fried in butter. A Tuesday that starts with salsa dancing and ends with Fernet shots on a stranger's balcony sounds like a TV show pilot, and maybe it should be. But stack enough of those Tuesdays and your writing career morphs into a very expensive gap year.

This is the paradox of power: when you can do anything, the discipline to do something becomes your rarest asset.

I've seen digital nomads who were clearly running *toward* something—mastery, momentum, meaning. I've also seen those sprinting *away* from ghosts: a toxic job, a hollow relationship, a sense of self they couldn't stomach. Distance feels like a solution until you remember that location doesn't rewrite your internal code. Wherever you go, your brain and your unique set of problems tags along like an overeager carry-on.

Let me be clear: I would never trade my five-year journey as a digital nomad for anything. The coffee shops of Seoul? A symphony of minimalist design and perfect Cherry Blossom NOLAs. The medieval core of Kraków, where my daily loop circled cobblestones older than America? Pure story fuel. And the Inca Trail? Twenty-six miles of stone steps and altitude that made me question every life choice, until Machu Picchu rose out of the mist like a hallucination built by gods. Those moments were worth every bout of jet lag or delayed flight.

But here's why I eventually parked the suitcase and built a home base in San Francisco: power without guardrails corrodes. After half a decade of relentless input—new cities, new languages, new sensory overload—my ideas needed stillness to coalesce. At some point, you trade the high of novelty for the deeper hit of mastery.

So say yes to the passport stamps. Book the ticket to Berlin or Singapore. But also know when to come home—whether home is an old Victorian in San Francisco or a borrowed desk in a friend's guest room. Build the habits and the friendships that tether you to meaning, not just momentum. Anchor before you drift into hedonistic purgatory where every day is a vacation and every draft dies on the runway.

Because here's the final twist: the greatest danger to freedom isn't poverty. It's apathy. The ability to do anything can quietly mutate into doing nothing. That's how empires crumble—not with a bang, but with a bottomless brunch and nights spent drinking to numb creeping feelings of doubt at bars.

Great power really does come with great responsibility, and in this case, that responsibility is to yourself. To your work. To the vision that launched you out of the cubicle and into the clouds in the first place. Don't let your hard-won freedom turn into a self-imposed exile. You fought for this latitude. Use it like a scalpel, not a sledgehammer.

Power Move: Design Your Freedom Season

Freedom without direction is chaos in disguise. Before you start booking flights or locking yourself into a home office, pause. Power is choice, but choice requires clarity.

Here's your power move:

1. **Name Your Season.** Ask yourself: What do I crave most right now? More novelty? Then maybe this is your "exploration season." More depth? Maybe it's your "creation season," focused on anchoring and deep work.
2. **Audit Your Energy.** Journal on this prompt: What activities make me feel most alive right now—movement, conversation, solitude, sensory overload? Your answers will hint at whether to pack a suitcase or a weighted blanket.
3. **Define the Why Behind the Where.** If you're itching to fly to Switzerland, great—but write down why. Is it because you want creative input, or because your business is secretly on fire and you're avoiding fixing the sprinkler system? Brutal honesty here prevents a lot of mid-air meltdowns.
4. **Build Your Guardrails.** Power erodes without structure. If you're going nomadic, schedule client deliverables, set hard office hours, and pick locations with strong Wi-Fi. If you're nesting at home, block deep work sprints and schedule local adventures or workout classes to get you out of the house so you don't rot in your sweatpants.
5. **Commit to a Reset Date.** Every season needs a horizon line. Decide when you'll reassess—three months, six months, a year. Mark it on your calendar. Power thrives on conscious recalibration.

There's no wrong answer to any of the above, but be sure not to fall into a default setting. Don't drift into someone else's dream writing life. Define your own, then execute with intention.

Amy's Field Notes: Boba, Dumplings, and a Lesson in Joy

The most magical trips rarely make it onto a spreadsheet.

Case in point: Taiwan. It wasn't on the itinerary. Kyle and I were mid-stay in Japan, staring down a rigid plan that suddenly felt stale. So we torched it. Booked last-minute flights to Taipei and landed with nothing but carry-ons and curiosity.

Kyle is a boba evangelist, so we decided to make the trip a pilgrimage: a full-blown boba crawl through the city that invented the drink. For the uninitiated, boba is tea loaded with chewy tapioca pearls, which is a textural adventure in a cup. In America it costs ten dollars. In Taipei? Just three.

We hopped from shop to shop in Taipei, scoring tea like Olympic judges, buzzed on caffeine and sugar, both of us pretending that prediabetes was a myth. Watching Kyle light up with every sip was pure dopamine. That secondhand joy—that's the stuff power buys. Not the tea, but the freedom to scrap the plan and chase whimsy without checking a PTO balance.

And because indulgence loves company, we hit the original Din Tai Fung not once, not twice, but *three* times in the same week. I have nothing profound to say about dumplings except this: nirvana comes in a bamboo basket, and going early on a Thursday afternoon to skip the line because you're not chained to a cubicle is the kind of quiet luxury that tastes better than truffle oil.

On our last day we hiked Elephant Mountain. Taipei stretched below us, a concrete sea wrapped in humid green, the skyline punctured by Taipei 101 like a jade spear. Fog rolled in as the sun folded itself into the horizon, and for a moment the city looked like a dream dissolving at the edges.

That's when it hit me: this entire chapter of my life—every rooftop bar in Singapore, every late-night ramen hunt in Kyoto, every accidental detour to Taipei—was bought with words. Lines I wrote in airports. Pages I drafted at dawn in strange cities. In that sense, these weren't vacations. They were dividends.

But here's the deeper note: these experiences aren't about the clout. They're about unlocking the more human side of power. Watching Kyle beam over a tapioca pearl. Meeting strangers who become lifelong friends. Eating dumplings that make you weep a little. This isn't about writing for money and power so you can buy another handbag or flex your wealth in a fancy car. It's about building a life rich with wonder before time runs out.

Because it *will* run out. I was reminded of that recently when a video crossed my feed of a 95-year-old woman saying goodbye to her husband on his death bed. The video punched me straight in the soul because life is an endless series of farewells. At the end of the day, we must say goodbye to everyone and everything we've ever loved.

But between the hello and the goodbye, we get choices. We get afternoons where the boba tea is fresh, the view is hazy, and the love of your life is laughing so hard you forget what decade it is.

That, not the bank account screenshot or the bestseller badge, is the payoff. That's what you're really writing for.

So go build that. Use the money and the power not just to pay bills, but to bankroll meaning. Use it to carve out those moments that make you whisper *holy shit* under your breath.

Because the only real metric that matters at the end is this: did you live wide open before the curtain fell?

Did you spend enough time with the people you loved, doing what you loved?

Or did you let gatekeepers and others' expectations of you dictate how you spend, as Mary Oliver once asked, "this one wild and precious life?"

CONCLUSION: WI-FI AND
WEAPONIZED WORDS

You're living in the single most extravagant moment a writer has ever occupied.

You, sitting there with a blinking cursor and a fully-charged laptop, have a global distribution system at your feet. One router. One "@" symbol. No need for ink-stained fingers or stacks of envelopes. Your words can slip into the pockets of readers who refresh their email while waiting in line for coffee.

Meanwhile, every empire that used to control audience access is cracking. Hollywood tried to save itself with streaming and accidentally underpriced writers to the point of strikes and existential meltdown. Traditional media execs openly admit their fiercest rival is free videos on social media filmed by creators who aren't anointed by the legacy systems.

Power is drifting out of the corner office and into the hands of anyone with Wi-Fi and something to say.

And gatekeepers know this. They're betting you won't figure it out. They're betting you'll stay hungry—literally and artistically. They'll spin the myth that money and technology corrupts art so you'll underprice your brilliance and stay obedient.

Spoiler: money is not a moral compromise. It's creative oxygen.

Cash pays for cover design, health insurance, therapy, research trips, and the 3 a.m. impulse to start a novella nobody greenlit but you.

And technology? These tools can help you create and distribute your work faster and better than ever before.

Power isn't about domination. It's about freedom: the right to say yes to work that thrills you and no to every vampire project draining you dry.

If these pages have done anything, I hope they've torched the ceiling you thought you had. I hope they've nudged you from thinking of writing as a "decent side hustle" and instead as a seven-figure writing business. That's not arrogance. It's an invitation.

So go write the story that feels too risky. Launch the paid tier of your newsletter. Quote the number that makes your voice shake. Hire your dream teammate. Send the cold email to the client who intimidates you.

And when you need your first (or next) writing job or pep talk, you can find me at MakeWritingYourJob.com or at Sutoscience.com. Every week my team and I share writing job roundups, success stories, and behind-the-scenes experiments—all the stuff I wish I'd had years ago.

Write for art. Write for fun. Write for rage. But don't be ashamed to write for money and power.

Money fuels the mission. Power protects the art. Earn both—then use them to kick the doors wide for the next generation of storytellers.

Now go write what only you can.

AUTHOR'S NOTE

Thank you so much for reading *Write for Money and Power*. The fact that you chose to spend your time with this book means a lot to me, truly.

If you found it valuable, here's one small action that makes a huge difference: leaving a review.

As a self-published author, I rely on readers like you to help this book make it into the hands of the writers who can benefit the most from it.

Every review you leave helps amplify this message and helps another writer escape the damaging starving artist myth. You never know what impact sharing this book can have on writers who are trying to stand confident in their skills and carve a better life for themselves.

So if something in here helped you—whether it was a single insight or the whole thing—I'd be grateful if you'd take a minute or two to write a short review and share with a writer friend.

Here are some links and QR codes to help you leave a review:

- Amazon

- Goodreads

If you want to stay in touch, you can also find me on Substack:

- Join my community for writers and access the writing job board at MakeWritingYourJob.com

- Learn how to grow your paid newsletter and attend my other classes at Sutoscience.com

See you around the writing world,
-Amy

BIBLIOGRAPHY

Martinez, Gerry. "Did Michelangelo Get Paid to Paint the Sistine Chapel?" GerryMartinez.com. Accessed 2025. https://www.gerrymartinez.com/did-michelangelo-get-paid-to-paint-the-sistine-chapel/.

Hooper, John. "Michelangelo's Sistine Chapel Paintings Were Work of Suffering Genius." The Guardian. Accessed 2025. https://www.theguardian.com/world/2002/nov/30/artsandhumanities.arts.

Writers Guild of America West. *Writer Employment Snapshot*. Accessed 2025. https://www.wga.org/uploadedfiles/the-guild/reports/WGA_Writer_Employment_Snapshot.pdf.

Galloway, Stephen. "Francis Ford Coppola Funded His $120 Million Film 'Megalopolis' with His Wine Business." Business Insider. Accessed 2025. https://www.businessinsider.com/francis-ford-coppola-funded-megalopolis-100-million-wine-business-2024-9.

Wikipedia contributors. "Hollywood Accounting." *Wikipedia*. Accessed 2025. https://en.wikipedia.org/wiki/Hollywood_accounting.

Adkins, Mary. "How Much Do Authors Make?" *Mary Adkins Blog*. Accessed 2025. https://maryadkinswriter.com/blog/how-much-do-authors-make.

PublishDrive. "What Are Book Advances? How Book Advances and Royalties Work." *PublishDrive Blog*. Accessed 2025. https://publishdrive.com/what-are-book-advances-how-book-advances-and-royalties-work.html.

Goldman Sachs. "The Creator Economy Could Approach Half a Trillion Dollars by 2027." *Goldman Sachs*. Accessed 2025. https://www.goldmansachs.com/insights/articles/the-creator-economy-could-approach-half-a-trillion-dollars-by-2027.

Santos, Emilia. "Utilizing Digital Vision Boards in Goal-Setting and Reflection." *ResearchGate*. Accessed 2025. https://www.researchgate.net/publication/391037151_Utilizing_Digital_Vision_Boards_in_Goal-Setting_and_Reflection.

Creswell, J. David, and Emily K. Lindsay. "How Does Mindfulness Training Affect Health? A Mindfulness Stress Buffering Account." *Psychological Bulletin* 144, no. 4

(2018): 692–730. Accessed 2025. https://www.ncbi.nlm.nih.gov/pmc/articles/PMC6220635/.

Ravikant, Naval. "Play long-term games with long-term people." *X (formerly Twitter)*. Accessed 2025. https://x.com/naval/status/1002103559276478464.

Zhou, Ying-Ying, et al. "Digital Detox: Disconnecting for Mental Health and Wellbeing." *International Journal of Environmental Research and Public Health* 21, no. 8 (2024): 1132. Accessed 2025. https://www.ncbi.nlm.nih.gov/pmc/articles/PMC11591838/.

Shakespeare Birthplace Trust. "How Much Was Shakespeare Worth?" *Let's Talk Shakespeare Podcast*. Accessed 2025. https://www.shakespeare.org.uk/explore-shakespeare/podcasts/lets-talk-shakespeare/how-much-was-shakespeare-worth/.

Biography.com Editors. "How Wealthy Was William Shakespeare?" *Biography.com*. Accessed 2025. https://www.biography.com/authors-writers/a64501905/william-shakespeare-wealth.

The Morgan Library & Museum. "A Letter from Charles Dickens." *The Morgan Library & Museum*. Accessed 2025. https://www.themorgan.org/collection/A-Letter-from-Charles-Dickens/44.

Docslib.org. "Charles Dickens and His Cunning Manager George Dolby Made Millions from a Performance Tour of the United States, 1867–1868." *Docslib.org*. Accessed 2025. https://docslib.org/doc/2286444/charles-dickens-and-his-cunning-manager-george-dolby-made-millions-from-a-performance-tour-of-the-united-states-1867-1868.

Eckstein, Katelyn. "How Heather Cox Richardson Built a Paid Newsletter with Over 1 Million Subscribers." *Growth in Reverse*. Accessed 2025. https://growthinreverse.com/heather-cox-richardson/.

Nelson, Jeff. "Author Ana Huang Is Twisting Up the Romance Genre — and Topping Best-Seller Lists Doing It." *People*. Accessed 2025. https://people.com/ana-huang-books-twisted-king-of-sloth-8630875.

Ducharme, Jamie. "Brené Brown on How to Be a Better Leader."*Time*. Accessed 2025. https://time.com/5441422/expert-feelings-brene-brown-leadership/.

Bishop, Rollin. "Brandon Sanderson's Kickstarter Campaign Becomes Most-Funded Publishing Project Ever." *Engadget*. Accessed 2025. https://www.engadget.com/brandon-sanderson-kickstarter-campaign-record-most-funded-091530765.html.

Page Six. "Taylor Swift Announces She Bought Back Her Masters with Heartfelt Note to Fans, 'Bursting into Tears.'" *Page Six*. Accessed 2025. https://pagesix.com/2025/05/30/entertainment/taylor-swift-announces-she-bought-back-her-masters-with-heartfelt-note-to-fans-bursting-into-tears/.

Wikipedia contributors. "The Eras Tour Book." *Wikipedia*. Accessed 2025. https://en.wikipedia.org/wiki/The_Eras_Tour_Book.

Weintraub, Karen. "How Hugh Howey Turned His Self-Published Story *Wool* into a Success & a Book Deal." *Writer's Digest*. Accessed 2025. https://www.writersdigest.com/be-inspired/how-hugh-howey-turned-his-self-published-story-wool-into-a-success-a-book-deal.

Wikipedia contributors. "Mere-Exposure Effect." *Wikipedia*. Accessed 2025. https://en.wikipedia.org/wiki/Mere-exposure_effect.

Wikipedia contributors. "A Tolkien Compass." *Wikipedia*. Accessed 2025. https://en.wikipedia.org/wiki/A_Tolkien_Compass.

Tolkien Gateway. "The Lord of the Rings Foreword." *Tolkien Gateway*. Accessed 2025. https://tolkiengateway.net/wiki/The_Lord_of_the_Rings_Foreword.

World Health Organization. "Burn-out an Occupational Phenomenon: International Classification of Diseases." *WHO.int*. Accessed 2025. https://www.who.int/news/item/28-05-2019-burn-out-an-occupational-phenomenon-international-classification-of-diseases.

Runn. "Burnout Statistics: 28+ Scary Stats and Facts." *Runn Blog*. Accessed 2025. https://www.runn.io/blog/burnout-statistics.

Wu, L. Fiona, Dashun Wang, and James A. Evans. "Research: When Small Teams Are Better Than Big Ones." *Harvard Business Review*. Accessed 2025. https://hbr.org/2019/02/research-when-small-teams-are-better-than-big-ones.

Oschinski, Jan, and Natalia Melnychuk. "Large Language Models as Job Search Engines: The Case of ChatGPT." *Scientific Reports* 14, no. 1 (2024). Accessed 2025. https://www.nature.com/articles/s41598-024-76900-1.

RECOMMENDED READING

- *Atomic Habits* by James Clear
- *The 4-Hour Workweek* by Tim Ferriss
- *$100M Offers* by Alex Hormozi
- *Essentialism* by Greg McKeown
- *Burnout: The Secret to Unlocking the Stress Cycle* by Emily and Amelia Nagoski
- *Year of Yes* by Shonda Rhimes

ACKNOWLEDGMENTS

First, thank you to Kyle Cords. You're my partner, my anchor, and the reason any of this is possible. You've always reminded me to come back to the basics, to return to the page, and to trust myself. Thank you for being part of my story. It's an honor to be part of yours, too. I'm endlessly grateful for your support, your patience, and for letting me turn moments from our life into stories that (hopefully) help other people. I can't wait to write our next chapter together.

To the MakeWritingYourJob.com community, thank you for being here. Watching you get your first writing jobs, grow your confidence, and build writing lives that actually work is the greatest privilege of my career. I built this book with you in mind. I've read every comment, every reply, every question you've posted in Subscriber Chat, and it all helped shape what this became. Thank you for trusting me. I'm so proud to be in your corner.

Thank you to my team, the behind-the-scenes magic makers who helped bring this book into the world.

Haley Raymond, thank you for being a thoughtful, strategic force of nature in the world of press and PR. Your clarity and care in getting this book out there has blown me away. I'm lucky to have you in my corner.

Renee Puvvada, thank you for helping me wrangle keywords, categories, Amazon weirdness, and every piece of the puzzle that turns a finished manuscript into a successful launch. I appreciate your brilliance more than you know.

Thank you to my beta readers: Sarah Aldrich, Yolanda Allen,

Faith Anderson, Agata Antonow, Robin Blanchard, Michele Bolton, Hanne Blank Boyd, Lauren Burke Meyer, Kristalynn Busskohl, Shelby Chambers, Cosette Chichirau, Liz Cooper, Edith Craig, Q El Crosby, Courtney Daniels, Estefania De La Concha, Jennifer Della'Zanna, Marie DeNoia Aronsohn, Marlene deWilde, Samantha Dobin, Cara Dolence, Kate Edenborg, Kristin Evans, Shernell Gary, Becca Glantz, Jodi Gonzalez, Ben Gran, Allison Grinberg-Funes, Justine Gunn, Claire Holden, Peter Holland, Lillian Jackson, Alexa Jordan, Shannon Jordan, Rebecca Landman, Andrea Lewis, Amy Martin, Isaura Martínez, Simoné Sanders McMurray, Amber Michelle, Sarah Mitchell, Sibylla Nash, Mai-anne Nguyen, Sandra Nyamu, Niha Pereira, Emily Pogue, Simon Presland, Renee Puvvada, Sabrina Reed, CaReese Rials, Trish Riley, Colleen Rivera, Tonya Rozelle, Willa Sears, Nilambari Shirodkar, Taylor Sievers, Luanna Stewart, Catherine Stockalper, Susan Treut, Andi Utter, Leon Vitale, Alyssa Wiens, Laura Michelle Wolff, Haley Wright, Joel Wukotich, and Carly York. Thank you for your feedback, generosity, and sharp insight. You made this book stronger, smarter, and clearer. I'm grateful for the time you gave to help this book succeed in its mission to making the writing world a better place.

Mom, Dad, and my brother: thank you for your unwavering support, even when I made what looked like insane choices. Like selling everything and traveling the world for five years. Or deciding not to go to law school. Or writing books with titles like *Write for Money and Power*. Thank you for standing by me when I chose the uncertain path, and for believing I'd find a way to make it work. You're the reason why I'm not a lawyer right now, and honestly what a gift that is.

And finally, to you, the reader. Thank you for choosing this book. It's not lost on me that in a world full of noise, you chose to spend your time here. That's a gift I don't take lightly. I remember what it was like to write without anyone on the other side. Writing for an audience is a different kind of magic. It's one I never take for granted.

If this book helped you and if it sparked something, challenged something, or opened a door, then that's all I ever wanted. I hope it gives you something worth carrying with you. I'll be back with another book soon.

ABOUT THE AUTHOR

Amy Suto is a former Hollywood TV writer turned seven-figure ghostwriter, bestselling author, and creator of the top-ranked Substack newsletter *Make Writing Your Job*. She's the author of *Write for Money and Power* and *Six-Figure Freelance Writer*, as well as the romantasy novel *The Ash Trials* and the short-story collection *The Nomad Detective: Volume I*. Based in San Francisco, Amy works with writers and high-net-worth clients to turn bold ideas into bestselling books and thriving creative empires. You can learn more about Amy at AmySuto.com.

ALSO BY AMY SUTO

The Ash Trials

Six-Figure Freelance Writer: A Holistic Guide on Finding Freedom in Freelancing

The Nomad Detective: Volume I

www.ingramcontent.com/pod-product-compliance
Lightning Source LLC
Chambersburg PA
CBHW071347210326
41597CB00015B/1564